Reinventing Capitalism

Jon Freeman

How we broke money and how we fix it, from inside and out

Reinventing Capitalism

Jon Freeman

How we broke money and how we fix it, from inside and out

Published by: SpiralWorld

www.spiralworld.net

© **Jon Freeman 2015**

ISBN 978–0956-0107-7-3   Paperback

ISBN 978–0956-0107-8-0   E-book and Kindle

i

Contents

Introduction

Imagine this.

You wake up one morning to find that money has gone. Mysteriously it has all vanished. Not just your money, which you notice when there are no coins or notes in your pocket or purse. All money. You are not having this experience alone. As news emerges over the next couple of hours it becomes clearer and clearer. There is no money any more, anywhere. It all disappeared at 5 a.m.

Your savings have all gone, but so have your mortgage and your credit card debts. Your bank balance is zero. All your accounts are zero. Your pension has ceased to exist. Your investment portfolio is valueless. Your employer doesn't know how to pay you. You don't know how to buy anything. Money has simply stopped, and with it all the relationships that you have been using money for.

At first these thoughts might feel scary. Your world seems paralysed. And yet, when you think about it, you are not under any immediate threat. You probably have food in your fridge or freezer. If not, a friend will probably give you a can of beans. Your loved ones and friends are still there. Your home has not vanished, and nor has your job. The TV still works and so does your phone. Right this minute, nothing has changed. The sun is still warming the earth, as much as it generally does. You are safe.

And then a few hours later it all changes. On the stroke of noon, money comes back, but not as before. You notice that you have exactly half what you had last night. A check of your online account shows that your balance has halved. Credit cards have done the same. The price display on your nearby garage shows half yesterday's price. All over the world there is half as much money as there was before.

And the world still hasn't changed at all. Not a brick, not a blade of grass. During that six hours people have been born and others have died, just as they always do. Life continued.

Money is not real. In this minute, right now, it could all disappear and we would still be here, still breathing. So how did money come to be so important? Why are business and economics such a mess? That is what this book is about. It's about the mystery of money, and how we solve it.

Re-inventing Capitalism?

I'm not saying either that economics is in good shape or that its flaws don't matter. It isn't, they do, and I'm all for rethinking and reforming a field.

The big problem with economic policy is not, however, that conventional economics doesn't tell us what to do. In fact, the world would be in much better shape than it is if real-world policy had reflected the lessons of Econ 101. If we've made a hash of things — and we have — the fault lies not in our textbooks, but in ourselves.

Paul Krugman. New York Times. September 2014

What would it take to be in contentment with money, economics and capitalism? What do our personal and planetary health, happiness, stability and sustainability require of us?

Money is one of the most important influences on human life, touching us all through our relationships with the resources we depend on. Alongside belief systems it is a leading cause of major conflicts.

You might think that this would have led to really good understanding of what money is and how to make it work for us. This book will show how far that is from the truth. You might also think that we would see the connection between how we relate to money as individuals, how we make businesses function, how we manage society and how the global economic system works. That doesn't appear to be true either.

There are many reasons to believe that money is not working well for us. Even without the credit crunch and the next imminently bursting bubble there are numerous causes for doubt. Inequality in society and across the planet, ecological and climatic sustainability, poor natural resource distribution and corruption are all visible issues. Money began as a tool to serve us – a way to make our relationships easier but the sense that money is no longer a tool that serves us is unavoidable. We have allowed it to become the master. The first question that is asked when a problem arises is no longer "What can we do?" Now we ask "Where will the money come from?"

This reflects a larger societal trend. Since the Age of Enlightenment we have had a very material view of existence, one which sees fragments and components but struggles to grasp whole pictures. Economists analyse the large-scale forces affecting national and global money-flows. Company board directors, bankers and investment analysts govern the future of our corporations. A few people have dabbled with the personal psychology of money, but the individual is not often seen as part of the equation. We are rolled up into collectives of consumer behaviour or industrial relations even though our views and our individual choices ultimately shape the economy. Each of these scales of operation is treated separately. The inner world of beliefs and value systems is not seen in relation to the outer manifestation of systems or structures.

We have survived this fragmentation until now because we lived in a slower, less interconnected and less complex world. Now we deal with multiple global interactions taking place at electron-speed at every scale. The result is unpredictability. Experts in complexity theory tell us how this chaotic turbulence means that small changes can cause large perturbations and major consequences. Books appear with titles such as "Tipping Point" and "Black Swans". It no longer works to yank the tiger's tail - to make our choices based on seeing parts of the system.

We know that we face major challenges. We depend on ecological systems that we don't understand and systematically damage. We deal with global warming, population growth, simultaneous famine and obesity, political instability and technological dependence on scarce resources at the same time as seeing exploitation and major wealth shifts from the poor to the richest. We could pray for Divine intervention or bury our heads and hope that it will magically work itself out. So far the indications are that this is an arena in which we are required to exercise our God-given intelligence and free will. That means we accept that humans created these problems and are required to solve them.

4

Some people already believe that we have already done too much damage and predict that the planet itself will deal with the drastic rebalancing. Whether through diseases which thrive on our overcrowding and lack of geographical containment, through major failures of food supply and water contamination, through direct conflict involving people with Iron Age thinking systems and access to 21st-century weaponry or through some even less predictable form of meltdown, it is conceivable that the global reset button will be pushed to reduce human numbers and human impact. Whether this is true or not, the demands on us are the same either way. The same responses are required to avert such catastrophes as to manage their aftermath. We have to get to grips with the entirety of what it takes to live as a global civilisation or we risk being propelled all the way back to the Middle Ages. You cannot operate cities with 10 million people except through the transport systems that bring in food and remove waste and the power grids that keep everything functioning. The planet cannot sustain 7 billion people with our current operating systems.

We must embrace unprecedented levels of connectedness in order to deliver the ways of functioning that our future is calling for. The views in this book and the proposals that it puts forward offer a framework and a conversation-starter for a redesign. That redesign connects our inner values to the challenges of existence that they are intended to help us meet.

All of the approaches, solutions and answers that we will need are already available to us but they are like scattered pixels or pieces of a jigsaw awaiting assembly. What is needed is a way to connect the dots or a table on which to lay out the jigsaw. This book offers a narrative for that connectivity and a way of joining the dots. It connects the individual relationship with money and the way that we view finance all the way up the scale through our societal expectations, our ways of operating and governing business, our national aspirations and our global connections, together with all the systems that we have built to facilitate these.

Is capitalism already dying?

There are those who would say that capitalism is already at an end – not for the reasons of imminent failure just given, but because it is being replaced. A typical example of this line of thought can be found in Paul Mason's Guardian article[i] (July 2015) heralding his book "Postcapitalism".

"As with the end of feudalism 500 years ago, capitalism's replacement by postcapitalism will be accelerated by external shocks and shaped by the emergence of a new kind of human being. And it has started.

Postcapitalism is possible because of three major changes information technology has brought about in the past 25 years. First, it has reduced the need for work, blurred the edges between work and free time and loosened the relationship between work and wages. The coming wave of automation, currently stalled because our social infrastructure cannot bear the consequences, will hugely diminish the amount of work needed – not just to subsist but to provide a decent life for all."

Similar expectations for the future have been voiced by Jeremy Rifkin. In books like "The Zero Marginal Cost Society" and "The Third Industrial Revolution: How Lateral Power is Transforming Energy, the Economy, and the World" he talks similarly about the effects of the internet, domestic power generation, 3D printing and other changes both in the means of production – from factories to workshops – and in the rise of knowledge economy, will *"usher in a fundamental reordering of human relationships, from hierarchical to lateral, that will impact the way we conduct commerce, govern society, educate our children, and engage in civic life."*

---

[i]   http://www.theguardian.com/books/2015/jul/17/postcapitalism-end-of-capitalism-begun?CMP=share_btn_tw

Paul Mason's argument draws on a wide range of phenomena – what the media has termed the "sharing economy" - involving creative commons, new forms of ownership and lending, collaborative and networked production and most of all, an information economy.   In his words *Today, the whole of society is a factory"*.

The title of Mason's article is "The end of capitalism has begun". However, he states that the new economic impulses and the old will co-exist for a long time. He says that it will need the state to create the framework and that the state, the (old) market and the collaborative new market will need to work together. I don't propose to disagree with Rifkin or Mason's predictions.   The trends they are referring to will support the propositions that this book will make. Nor would I question Mason's assertion that these trends will make the old forms of socialist thinking even less relevant. In its own way this book will support his assertion of the need to "build alternatives within the system". That is already happening.   Even so, there are many aspects of the current system which urgently need re-shaping. The new economic impulses do not change that, and how we think and feel about money will also remain central to who we are and how we act.

Why not ditch capitalism?

There is a trap waiting for the unwary writer who uses the word "Capitalism". It is almost as fraught as using the word "love". With love, at least people are broadly in favour of it even if there is a need to clarify what kind of love we are talking about.

Since we all know that there are things about our money system that are not working many would completely identify our current challenges with Capitalism. Capitalism itself is Bad and Wrong For others, to use the word when looking to the future implies constraints, causing concerns that we will not be free to do whatever is required to birth something new. They wish to avoid any possibilities being taken off the table.

For many people and most particularly for those who currently have money or political power anything that questions Capitalism is an instant recipe for closed ears, hearts and minds. It is taken to imply an intention to destroy the system. For some that may instantly be assumed to mean that something like Socialism, Communism or Anarchy is being proposed. Neither of these apply here. I align with the view of Sudhakar Ram, author of "The Connected Age" that Adam Smith's notions of perfect competition are still waiting to be applied with perfect integrity.

It is legitimate to go further than this. In looking at how the system has operated for the last several decades we will see that we have not had a capitalist system at all. What we have had is a debtist system. The way we operate money these days does not rely on genuine capital. It is based not on the creation of real wealth – goods, services and human well-being – but on the expansion of numbers. The vast majority of those numbers represent debt.

This book has a cover image of bicycles. The first bicycle was the penny-farthing, hard to pedal or steer, uncomfortable and hard to balance. Over time it was improved and superseded by equal wheel-sizes, chain drives, gearing systems and calliper brakes. Today, bicycles can have rechargeable electric motors, light-alloy frames, sprung suspensions and multiple shapes. They may be foldable to combine with use of public transport. There was never anything wrong with the concept of "bicycle" or with the word itself and the journey was one of continuous improvement. Even now I could buy an electric motor kit to fit to my previous generation bike. Diversity of response and adaptation to varying usage requirements is part of the concept.

It is in this spirit that I use the title "Re-inventing Capitalism". Whatever suggestions this book leads to and whichever of the many ideas for improvement are eventually taken up, we will need to work with what we already have. This is more difficult than a redesigned bike because we are riding it all the while. We need to retain our balance and movement even as we change it, since the alternative is to be face-down in a ditch.

How do we know what the redesign calls for?

The fundamental thesis of this book is that the capitalism we have now was designed according to the beliefs and values we had at the time, the awareness we had of how the world functions and in the context of a world before globalisation, computerisation and multiple sustainability challenges. We built a system according to what we knew then and take it for granted that this is how it has to work. Meanwhile we are experiencing the discomfort, imbalance and steering challenges. Money isn't serving us well and seems to determine our direction more than our own choices do. Changing our minds about what we want from the system will not fix those problems. The system itself is as much a constraint as fixed pedals would be.

The beliefs and values relate to our perception of what money is and how it works, so the first part of the book is about our relationships with money, how they evolved and what they became. A new relationship with money will define the new beliefs and values that must drive the system redesign. To avoid repeating the previous design errors we must understand the mystery of money better than we do now. This section examines those values and how they led us to the edge of meltdown

How we currently use money reflects what we have been led to believe about how it is intended to function. We have to take a look at the fundamentals of what money systems must be capable of. The second part of the book explores the flaws that we have built in to our money system in more depth so that we can see the underlying principles of what we need it to do. It is here that we meet the core of the debtist system. It might be said that we need not so much to reinvent capitalism as to reinstate it.

The third part of the book places what we have discovered about money alongside the knowledge we have of today's world and its challenges. What kind of new bicycle is needed – an off-roader, a racing machine or a BMX? How many gears and what kind of tyres will fit our desired use and the conditions in which we are riding? What changes are being called for and how flexible can

9

we make them? Section 4 summarises the changes in a more concise form so that we have some sort of compass and a rudimentary map to start from. It is at least the starting point for a table on which to lay down the jigsaw puzzle.

Throughout the book we will see that the next stage with money and Capitalism is just one more step in an evolutionary journey. We have survived the others and we can thrive beyond this one. This book does not propose destroying the current system but neither does it believe that the possibilities for change are constrained, except in the sense that evolution can only ever work forward from what already exists. Humans are, after all, still formed from the same kind of single cells that first appeared billions of years ago. Those cells discovered how to assemble in their trillions and collaborate in large organisms with high levels of biological intelligence that we don't even have to think about. We breathe, digest, move and do whatever we do.

Now life requires us to adapt into an economic existence in which billions of us can display a similar level of collective functional intelligence. Even a butterfly starts with the imaginal cells in the material from the caterpillar. The genes are already there. Whatever species of economic being we evolve into next, we are still likely to use money. We are still likely to need to invest our resources to create new ventures. We are still likely to work with the same tensions between freedom to profit from creativity and inventiveness, and the way in which we express the human togetherness through caring and sharing. We will still need to circulate money and distribute other resources. More than ever we will need to deal with the ways in which we create war and societal conflict. The system by which we accomplish this needs re-invention, upgrade and re-release, but we can still call it Capitalism.

Section 1: How did we get into this mess?

Central to the Economics of Contentment is the general commitment to laissez faire. This is not a formally avowed principle – or in any case it is not so often affirmed. Rather, it is an attitude, the belief that it is in the nature of things, and especially of economic life, that all works out best in the end. Nothing that happens in the short run is in conflict with the longer-run well-being. ….

Contentment sets aside that which, in the longer view, disturbs contentment; it holds firmly to the thought that the long run may never come. ….

John Kenneth Galbraith. "The Culture of Contentment".

The economics of the future are different. You see, money doesn't exist in the 24th Century…The acquisition of wealth is no longer the driving force in our lives. We work to better ourselves and the rest of humanity.

Jean-Luc Picard. Star Trek. "First Contact"

1. The Mystery of Money

But godliness with contentment is great gain. For we brought nothing into this world, and it is certain we can carry nothing out. And having food and raiment let us be therewith content. But they that will be rich fall into temptation and a snare, and into many foolish and hurtful lusts, which drown men in destruction and perdition. For the love of money is the root of all evil: which while some coveted after, they have erred from the faith, and pierced themselves through with many sorrows. But thou, O man of God, flee these things; and follow after righteousness, godliness, faith, love, patience, meekness.

Letter of Paul to Timothy. Ch. 6, 6-11

What is money for? Why did we invent it?

When humankind first appeared on the earth, we do not picture him with a pocket full of money. We don't even picture him with pockets. Money did not physically evolve; we invented it.

The point of money is to facilitate human relationships. Some people would tell you that the first relationships were celebratory, that cowrie shells were used as a means of passing wealth when a marriage took place. Others would describe more directly commercial reasons, relating to trade. Our word "pay" is said to come from the Latin "pacare", meaning to pacify, as in settlement of a wrong.

Glyn Davies, in the book "A history of Money" describes it like this:-

"Money originated very largely from non-economic causes: from tribute as well as from trade, from blood-money and bride-money as well as from barter, from ceremonial and religious rites as well as from commerce, from ostentatious ornamentation as well as from acting as the common drudge between economic men."

In summary, since money was invented to facilitate human relationships it should be seen as a tool. It is something that we made to serve us, something that we should have mastery over.

That may not match your experience of money though. Few individuals show signs of being masters of money and the world as a whole transparently has no mastery at all. Money does not seem to serve us, quite the reverse. It seems to have enslaved us. You may also feel that it is a very unkind master, one with no feeling, no sympathy, no consideration and no human warmth. Perhaps it is time for this slavery to be abolished.

Money and Time

I want to make a fresh suggestion that adds to our definition of money. If we think of how things were before money, relationships typically operated in present time. Here and now I would make a trade with you, barter my two goats for your cow. In theory I might agree to receive your cow later (e.g. after she has calved). I might even give you two goats in the understanding that you would repay me in some appropriate way at a later date. In a typical pre-money society one would expect that such agreements would be enforced within the culture, through elders or community pressure, and before a long time had elapsed.

It is easy to see that money would always replace barter for many reasons. If you want my two goats and I don't want your cow but need ten sacks of wheat, it might be hard to find someone who is seeking a cow and has ten sacks of wheat. Money facilitates more complex interactions. It also allows us to determine relative values more easily. If you think your cow is worth two point four goats we're in difficulty and so maybe are the goats. Lastly goats and cows are not very portable forms of currency. Once society grows beyond very simple levels of transaction, a portable means of mediating exchange is an inevitable invention.

Initially that mediator is something that cannot be consumed, is quite scarce and is of perceived value in the culture – shells, precious stones or even gold. Eventually money – manufactured coins - are a logical development. The paper form that we are familiar with is not itself of any value. It is a promise to pay with something that is of value. On a British note you can read this clearly. At the top, the bank of England says "I promise to pay the bearer, on demand, the sum of ££" and the promise is signed by its chief cashier. Other currencies may not use these words on their notes, but all embody the same principle. At a time when we are all talking about "deficits" this is a reminder that all our money is a form of debt. I wonder what would happen if a thousand people marched on the Bank of England and asked them to pay out on their promise. What would they do? Would they give us cowrie shells? But I digress. Debt is a subject for later and we are talking about time.

The invention of a means of mediation changes our relationship with the world in a significant way. Before money, the things I owned had real value. I could milk my goat, breed from or even eat my goat. In the here and now I have a direct relationship with the world. If I breed from my goat and rear the kid to adulthood I have increased my wealth. But I have also changed the real world. I have added value to it, a goat which did not exist before.

With money I have a new possibility. Having reared my new goat I can sell it for money. I am rewarded for my work in animal husbandry. But the money I receive in return for my goat did not in itself add to the value of the world. It merely represents that value. And I can keep that representation in my pocket, or hide it in a hollow tree indefinitely. If the goat dies tomorrow and is lost to the world, I still have the money.

This is Lesson 1. There is no fixed relationship between the amount of money in the world and the amount of real value.

So, with the invention of money, we separate value from the here-and-now reality and we create the possibility of a relationship across time. To make this implication clearer, let's look at a few examples.

- I do not have to use my money. I can keep it "for a rainy day" or to give to my grandchildren.

- If I use my money to buy a service like a haircut, my money passes to the hairdresser. She does not keep the hair, and I have less of it. Any value in this transaction is a matter of perception, not physical reality. The hairdresser however can now purchase something real – a nice meat pie perhaps from the shop below.

15

- If I use the money to top up my phone, I give it to the phone company in return for a service that I receive in the future.

So far, so good. None of that looks too risky. I am using money that I already have in a variety of ways. All of those uses are largely under my control. So what about borrowing?

- I have forgotten my wallet and borrow the price of my lunch from you, to pay back tomorrow.

- My car tyre is punctured. I don't have the cash to fix it. I borrow a larger sum which I will not be able to pay back until the next pay day.

- My car fails its annual check and has to be replaced. I take out a

> *You can't put your Visa bill on your American Express card*
>
> *P.J. O'Rourke in "The Bachelor Home Companion"*

moderate twelve-month loan.

- I borrow to finance new equipment which increases the capability of my business and will generate the growth in revenue with which to repay

This is still reasonably under control with a low element of risk. Now we get to the trickier examples.

- I really fancy a flash car with real "pulling power". I take out a 3-year loan at high value.

- The car worked, and got me the woman of my dreams. I am marrying, starting a family and want to buy a house. I take out a 95% mortgage which will take me 25 years to pay off. I also max out my credit cards on honeymoon and furnishings.

- We've been married a couple of years, we are just about making ends meet. Credit cards are still maxed out. I'm a freak for technology and 3D TV's are on the market. I must have one and buy it on a credit agreement - the day before my wife tells me we're expecting.

It's fairly obvious that matters are now getting out of control, and the risk levels are increasing. Perhaps you can see your own experience in this escalation, or at least echoes of times when you have thought like this or behaved like it. If not, you certainly have seen it in others. When it goes wrong we treat it as really quite normal. It's just the way of the world and can't be helped. There's nothing really wrong, it is just that sometimes even intelligent people misjudge the situation. And some are feckless.

But we would miss what is really happening if it seems that this is simply about the management of money. We have already seen that money can distance us from the realities of the material world. When we borrow, it disconnects us from time.

When I borrow the money for my lunch, I may well pay back the following day. When we take out bank loans we start to extend to 3-year payback terms. Mortgages may take half our adult lives. More than that, we enter into a pattern where we are never living in "current time". We are always living in the future.

This is Lesson 2. Borrowing money equates quite literally to living on borrowed time.

What is debt?

In a world that has not yet invented money the capacity for debt is limited. I can borrow your axe. I can borrow your ox to pull my plough. Slightly less tangible, I can even borrow your time, if you help me with a task today. But the expectation is that your physical possessions are returned, and even the day of work is to be paid back soon. Perhaps the most extended view of this is that I can lend you some seed corn, expecting that you pay me back when harvest time comes. Of course life is uncertain; crops may fail this year. But such arrangements are generally short-term.

Our modern approach to debt is much more complex than this and we will examine it in greater detail as we go as it will be at the centre of many aspects of the money relationship. For now I will suggest that we note that debt has moved from the realm of person-to-person obligation and has become an institution. Debt is inbuilt to our lives, to how we expect to live. It is fundamental to all commerce and to the operation of the industrial and commercial worlds.

Since as noted, all money is "a promise to pay", you can also see that all money represents a debt. One of the traps in our relationship to money is that when you have money in your pocket it brings a kind of illusion with it. It seems as if you own something, as if money is something that you can "have". That illusion is sustained by the day-to-day expectation that if there is something you want, you can hand over your money to a shop and be given that thing in exchange. But never forget that what you handed over was someone else's promise to pay you. Their promise is now to pay the shopkeeper. What you passed on was someone's debt to you.

What is involved then, when money is borrowed? Ultimately, you receive a promise to pay you. To avoid getting your brain completely scrambled, it might help to think of receiving this in paper money, with the words "promise to pay the bearer" written on it. So you receive a pile of promises. You then make your own promise to pay that back (e.g. an IOU or loan agreement). When you do so, you will pay it back using another pile of promises to pay you.

Lesson 3. The system consists of us all making promises to each other.

There is a reason why we work this way and it is not completely irrational to operate this system. We don't want to go back to barter. We built the system to serve us. Unfortunately the system has weaknesses. The way that we are living now has exposed those weaknesses. It may seem that those weaknesses merely consist of banker greed and stupidity, of crazy risks and mad bonuses. But those symptoms are the tip of an iceberg. The block of ice that lifts it above the surface is something that you and I agreed to. We are still agreeing to it. It comes from us. It's a way of life and a way of thinking that has been turned into a system. Much of this book is about how and why we built that system, why the

18

weaknesses have gone beyond sustainability, and what we must do to have money be our friend, our helper, and not our master.

Summary Nuggets

Money is not real and is not connected to anything real unless we make it so.

Borrowed money and debt are money taken from present time into the future

Money appears to be payment, but is only ever a promise to pay later with something more real than money is.

2. The Evolution of Money

Fear, Mr. Bond, takes gold out of circulation and hoards it against the evil day. In a period of history when every tomorrow may be the evil day, it is fair to say that a fat proportion of the gold dug out of one corner of the earth is at once buried again in another corner.

Ian Fleming's "Goldfinger" (1959)

Following on from eons of biological change, human evolution now takes place socially and psychologically. While the gradual physiological adaptations are presumably continuing as they have done over millennia, the pace of such change is too slow to be detectable over a few thousand years. While our ways of life are significantly different from those of the ancient Egyptians or the classical Greeks, there is no obvious reason why a baby born to the pyramid-builders could not have been brought up in modern London or New York and have functioned successfully as a stock market trader.

Money on the other hand, has evolved. It is a social creation and has changed over time. In the first chapter we looked briefly at its origins as a means of exchange and its purpose as a facilitator of relationships. But the types of relationship themselves have changed as society has developed and it will help us to see the pattern that underlies those changes.

The dynamics of social change

According to the theory "Spiral Dynamics" originally formulated by Professor Clare W. Graves, then named and developed further by Dr. Don Beck, human beings evolve psychologically in such a way as to adapt to the life conditions they must deal with. For a primitive hunter-gatherer the focus is entirely towards survival. The band must eat, must protect itself from the elements and from predators. Their world is different from ours and they think differently. Status, for instance, has no value to them. He who dies with the most toys has lost, and his family may well die with him. The only laws that matter are the laws of the natural world. In a crisis (for example when hurricane Katrina devastated New Orleans in 2005) modern man will jettison those toys and ignore all statutes. He will fight for access to food, and shelter; he will loot shops. The life conditions change, and what we value changes with them.

Spiral Dynamics is rich and complex, but for our purposes here we can look at a small portion of the theory, starting with the forces which drive change in how humans think and live. One very visible force is the growth in societal scale. There is development from hunter bands, through settled tribes, to feudal warlords who rule whole regions. You can still find a few tribal societies living the old ways, and the politics of Afghanistan still displays its feudal roots. But most regions also show the later developments of towns and metropolitan cities, and in the Western world we can talk of global economics. Such growth in social scale is associated with continual change in our ways of thought and our Values systems. Money systems are built in to these changes.

Increased Societal Scale calls for different ways with money

A second force which drives societal adaptation is the need to balance the things that are of value to the individual with the needs of a social group. Society swings back and forward between our human desire to express ourselves and our liking for connection and togetherness. Money is used differently at different stages. When we get too far out of balance there is social discomfort and pressure to pull back. We reflect this in our attitudes to money, and in how we use it. Understanding of these forces tells us a great deal about the state of our world now, as we shall see.

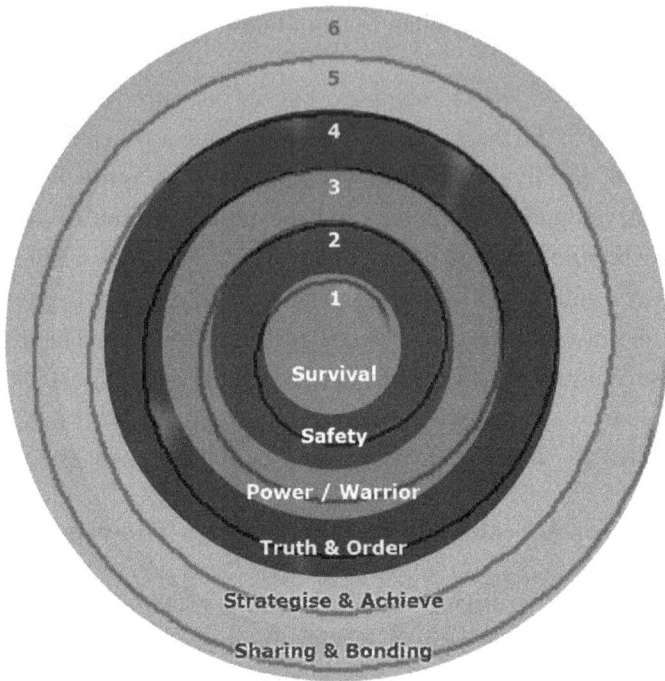

Stages 1 to 6 Nested

We must understand one more crucially important thing about this developmental process. Each stage is built on and includes the one that went before. The degree of inclusion varies, but it will become quite obvious as we describe the stages of development that by the time that we reach Stage 6, that it can only exist because of the support it receives from Stages 4 and 5. Stages do not replace each other and what we will see are nested systems within systems. So let's look at what money represents at different stages in the human journey, and what values are attached to it.

The social value of money

The first stage in human existence, the **survival** band stage, does not use money. But as humans began to be more successful and to grow in numbers, they could see that larger groups would bring **safety, thus in the second stage** tribes formed. Many tribes would still not use money, operating with gift relationships and mutual care / obligation, but the earliest developments would seem to have reflected the need to support social cohesion. Money was developed as a way to facilitate life's transition ceremonies and to cement social alliances such as through marriage dowry systems and ways to deal with death and inheritance.

Tribal societies tend to develop fixed systems, doing things as the ancestors did them, obeying the tribal elders and doing it "our way". This brings great stability but such constraints on expansion and initiative eventually become too great, and these pressures ultimately trigger a more individual and competitive thrust. This may also arise as one tribe comes into proximity with another, with different traditions and competing ways. For the leaders, "our way" becomes "my way" in relation to other leaders. The third stage is about who has **power;** it is the consciousness of the **warrior** in both its positive and negative senses. Money is used like other goods as a way of plunder and to express and display that power over others. At its best it is also expressed as power to create and it may finance heroic ventures too. At this stage, precious metals and jewels express not just a means of exchange, but the visible signs of power, capacity and influence.

When traders are always coming to blows, it is bad for business. When warlords are overthrown a whole family may be massacred in order to prevent revenge. The pressures rise for a more stable way to manage. This too is influenced by increasing numbers. The transition that takes place is the one exemplified by Genghis Khan's Mongol empire in the 12th century or by the earlier growth of the Roman Empire, subduing the Celts, Gauls etc. under the "pax romana". Gradually as humans move into Stage 4, **order** is imposed, laws are made and there is some collective agreement. Many of the laws regulate the ways that trade, commerce and money usage take place. Here in stage 4, written systems are likely to come into greater use.

Up to stage 3 only the physical money was of significance, since possession was the law. In this fourth stage, we are more likely to see the use of tally systems and of written agreements that are enforceable by collective law rather than by simple "because I say so" power. Money is at the centre of social order and stable societies allow expansion in trading relationships. It is the beginning of money as we know it; however the boundaries are not clean and simple between the stages. For instance, the time of Elizabeth I would show some internal order, but the external relationship with the Spanish allowed piracy, stealing gold from the Spanish ships. This balance, showing both power and order aspects, lasted for several hundred years.

As Clausewitz famously said, war is diplomacy by another means, and by the time of Queen Victoria, the British Empire had extended its dominance over much of the globe. Order is important, underwritten by the virtues of a Christian God and biblical values, but it is built on the foundation of military power, and brings a great deal of money back to Britain, which becomes a major centre of trade, commerce and banking. During these centuries, North America was colonised as an extension of French and British Empires, growing a parallel economic strength. You might say that commerce is war by another means, and sometimes vice versa..

One of the things that inspired my love of Spiral Dynamics is that the patterns it reveals are easily recognised. The picture of history that is being painted here not only fits our understanding of our own history, it also fits well to what is happening elsewhere in the world. The development of African countries, the differences between Israeli and Palestinian cultures and the transitions taking place in South America can all be mapped in this way. But the theory is not merely about history. It is about human social dynamics, so it is also predictive. It tells us where we are now, and the direction that we are moving in.

The Western World was moving through Stage 4 for a few centuries, and those ordering Values continue to provide foundations for today's world. Legal institutions, police forces, accountancy practices, legislatures and government administrations are the bedrock of modern society. But order and regulation can also behave like constraint and restriction. Humans are inventive and have the desire to express their capacity to create. At its worst, Stage 4 can generate police states or religious inquisitions. But even at its best, individuality will assert itself; the old order will be unsatisfactory to some and new impulses will be expressed. In our Western world history that emerges as the industrial revolution and the growth of global commerce. Stage 4 has prepared the way, developing a written culture and supporting the growth of education, leading to breakthroughs in science and engineering. In the 19th Century we saw the rise of manufacturing industry, railways and international trade. The C20th brought automotive and aircraft industries, telephony and electronics leading later to space exploration, global computerisation and the internet. These are the fruits of Stage 5.

> *Look at me. Worked myself up from nothing to a state of extreme poverty*
>
> *S.J. Perelman (via Groucho Marx) in film "Monkey Business"*

This too is a recognisable here-and-now story. Stage 5 thinking is individualistic and assertive, but rather than starting wars, it is **strategic**. The goal is more to **achieve** than to dominate. There is plenty of competition, but in this stage the aim is more strategic than the stage 3 warrior mentality and tries not to upset others too far, or not as far as to invite retribution. For people whose Values are centred in this stage, winning is important, and one of our most accepted ways to keep score is MONEY. Stage 5 loves toys and prestige, and these are both purchased with money. For individuals who hold these core values, it may not even be about the exact amount of money involved. As a banker, my million dollar bonus is enough when I know that my colleagues all received $900,000. If just one of them got $1.1M, then my million was inadequate. More than the latest prestige toy, money is what tells us we are winning.

As we have progressed through the stages thus far, the relationship between money and the underlying reality has been relatively stable. For a long time this was represented quite physically in the world. Currencies had their value underwritten by gold. The famous Fort Knox held large quantities of bullion, stacks of very heavy gold bricks. The "promise to pay" was in theory a promise to deliver the appropriate amount of that gold, and when currencies were bought and sold, gold would be physically moved from one vault to another. In 1966 it was estimated that over half the gold ever extracted from the ground was held in such vaults, and about 38,000 tonnes of it in America.

It is now four decades since President Richard Nixon abolished the Gold Standard, which tied the value of the dollar to that precious metal. We will look at the reasons for this later, but for now it is useful to take note of a significant shift that it represents. From this point on, money becomes its own reference point, and the aspiration to link it to physical reality has been broken. This allows the Stage 5 values system to make a focus of money itself. Since then, some of the creativity which propelled the industrial and technological age to make goods has been diverted into finding ways to make money. Not to make money as an outcome of creating goods and services, but rather to make money by growing the money itself as once we grew crops, to make "money-culture" the successor to agriculture. This will be central to understanding our future. It also relates to the triggering of Stage 6.

Living for ourselves, valuing possessions and money, competing with others can become unsatisfactory in a few ways. One is that it tends to lead to stress, and to dissatisfaction with what we have. We move away from family and friends if that is what it takes to "get on". Our attitude to relationships can become focussed on what others can do for us. In stage 4 even well-off individuals got married for the traditional partnership and children reasons. In the peak of stage 5 marriages can be like a corporate merger or possibly an acquisition, with status, lifestyle and economic implications. Stage 5 needs pre-nuptial contracts and complex divorce settlements.

For those who are not winning, the competition can lead to depression, loneliness and alienation, with alcohol or drugs either recreational or prescription in the wings. Even for the winners, recreational drugs may be part of the achiever lifestyle, as illustrated to the hilt in the film "Wolf of Wall Street". But underneath is the recognition that none of these fill the need which all humans have for connection. Even having children may not meet this need when they are in front of the TV, and finding the money for a desired lifestyle requires two working parents, possibly with long commutes. Many will feel the quiet promptings of other values like sharing and fairness. Consumption can feel very empty.

Whether from unfairness, loneliness or dissatisfaction, there is a pull back towards human values. Orderliness and stability are no longer enough and achievement has become empty. Flourishing in these conditions seems to demand that we find something in ourselves and each other. Stage 6 requires that we care for each other and that we understand more about our humanity. In historical terms, the industrial revolution triggers the rise of psychology and the welfare state. In the UK, the old-age pension (1908), unemployment benefit (1911) and a national health service (1948) come into being, paid for by the rising surplus that technology can deliver. At a simplistic level, the washing machine freed women to become nurses, social workers and teachers.

As a result, Stage 6 has a new use for money. Money is built in to the Stage 4 stability and order systems and it is a major motivator for individuals living from Stage 5 Values. But in Stage 6 it has an additional function as a means for **sharing and bonding**. It funds our welfare systems, it is redistributed by progressive taxation mechanisms. Stage 6 Values may be built on top of the achiever goals at Stage 5, but one of the ways to achieve status in the 5-6 transition would be by showing how much of our money we could give away.

Meanwhile there has been another outcome of technology. Transportation, industrial water, sewerage and power grids enable more people to live in cities. Food can be brought in from miles away. This takes resources which we are only just beginning to tally up. The concept of "food miles" is a recent one, but our entire urban lifestyle rests on a wide base of consumption, and brings associated problems with waste disposal. The majority of our garbage consists of packaging.

Money is affected by all the factors we have encountered so far. Cities are very complex systems which are highly dependent on the technological infrastructure. They may seem geographically self-contained but their economies spread far and wide. In addition, all the forces and Values that are represented in this story can be found inside Cities. There, people are surviving in cardboard-box houses, living in ethnic tribal groups and fighting gang wars,

27

as well as the more obvious ordering, commercial and social service functions. Cities and their problems provide a mirror for our planetary state. We are dealing with large numbers – many cities of above a million people – accompanied by diversity, complexity and external resource dependency.

Stage	Keywords	Values	Economy
1	Survival	Whatever it takes to stay alive in an unsafe world	Hand to mouth. Daily needs for food and shelter
2	Tribal Safety	Banding together for safety, with allegiance to elders, ancestral traditions and the natural world	Money, if present, to mark celebrations and cement family ties
3	Power	Expressing individual being through heroic achievement, self-gratification and power. Finding a place in a competitive pecking order ruled by the strong	Money as display and to pay for extravagant pleasures
4	Order And Purpose	Bringing our life together under the governance of laws, creating formalised hierarchies of command and control backed by the authority of the state or God	Money managed by formal agreements, accounting systems, banks and corporate entities
5	Modernism Strategy	Expressing individuality through innovation and, creativity, excellence, rewarding it through visible status and measurable tokens of achievement	Money as the propulsion for growth and the means of keeping score
6	Sharing and Human Bonding	Recognising the value of our humanness and the way that we are bonded in our shared human experience. Promoting fairness, social justice and care for the weak	Money diverted into elder care, socialised medicine and redistributed through taxation

The crisis

Because of this we are reaching a crisis point in our use of money. Above, we noted that the fundamental dynamics in human social evolution require continual adaptation to increasing complexity and ongoing balance between the "I" and the "We", the social and the individualising impulses within us. Our life conditions are showing that there is a "we" that is bigger than our own social groups – bigger even than our nations. Climate change, ecological damage, peak oil and energy security, food and water supply, population pressures and political conflicts are all bringing pressure points, none of them independent from the others. Collectively we are struggling at a global level to develop Value systems which meet these life conditions. Our money system reflects that. We will see that it is not fit for today's purposes, still less for tomorrow. The new "I" is our human species, which we all have an interest to preserve. The "We" is now an entire planet, where we have left it until the last minute to recognise our interdependence with other species and nature's gifts.

The requirement for our money system is now that it must **sustain** all of the first six stages and more. We still need inheritance systems and tribal cohesion. We still need the ability to balance power structures and support great individual endeavours. We need stability, order, infrastructure and regulation at the same time as enabling inventiveness and technological problem-solving. Nor can we let go of our social and health care systems. On top of this our money system must first align and then integrate all of the previous stages, enabling the flexibility and responsiveness that are needed to manage global complexity and interdependence through a critical transition.

To the extent that societies evolve, they increasingly become more complex until they are at a point where they can not manage the complexity any longer.

Professor Joseph Tainter, Universidad Nacional Autónoma de México,

The "credit crunch" has kindled a new awareness of financial balance and of what can go wrong when our money system loses touch with reality. The introduction of a carbon tax shows that we are beginning to think about the financial value of the planet itself, and the whole concept of "peak oil" is based on the recognition that long before it actually runs out, we reach the point where it costs more to extract than we can afford to pay. Fracking has merely postponed this, possibly at uncounted ecological cost which would even now make it truly unaffordable. Many of the material resources that we have blithely plundered will face this pressure at some point.

Above all, the view we have presented here of how our money systems evolve displays an interaction between our Values systems - what we think is important to our lives – and the ways that we perceive and use money. To see the future of money and to understand how we come through the crisis is a journey along the parallel strands of the material reality and the thoughts and feelings we hold about it. Change is needed both in the money system and in ourselves, but it won't change unless we do.

Lastly, the original purpose of money was to facilitate human transactions. Whether that transaction was a stage 2 ceremony, a stage 3 display of power or a stage 4 trade, money was for a purpose. It was to be used. But as Stage 4 developed, a new expectation arose whereby money itself could be required to grow. Stage 3 had vaults, treasuries and tallies. Written records enabled accounting systems, paper money and above all the mathematics of interest. From this point forward the idea of money turns into the notion of capital, embedding a system where those who already have money can make that money work for them. Money has hitherto been a reward for work done or for successful plunder of the work of others. Capitalism makes that money itself work, perpetuating the hierarchical structures and extending them through the generations. It then propels stage 5, where capital is held, not just in land, buildings, livestock and cash but spread into industrial and commercial ventures, further and further away from the owners of that capital. Throughout this transition, money shifts from being the result of power and increasingly becomes the source of power. As my friend Marcos observed, this can cause us to feel that our creativity, love, wisdom, generosity and compassion are no longer of value.

After Stage 6 in the Spiral journey we enter a new phase, a second tier of Value systems which call for us to manage the first tier 6-stage collective. We will see as we go forward that the nature of a complex, global and fast-changing world cannot achieve financial balance via our old Values, thinking or money systems. The changes we now require call for new relationships with power, both in ourselves and in what we are calling for from others. This brings an additional level of challenge to the undertaking, and provokes some very basic emotional reactions. We must understand and prepare for these.

Summary Nuggets

Over time, society has evolved its view of what money is, how we use it and how we think about our relationships with it.

In that evolution money changed from being a means to facilitate transactions towards being something that we gave an identity of its own and eventually into a commodity that could be developed in its own right.

The changes in thinking systems and in money are a response to increased complexity of the life conditions and relationships it is required to represent.

3. Fear and Greed

Capitalism is the extraordinary belief that the nastiest of men for the nastiest of motives will somehow work for the benefit of all.

John Maynard Keynes

Society drives people crazy with lust and calls it advertising

John Lahr

In our relationship with money, few of us live in total emotional comfort. To be reading this book, you must by definition be in some degree of physical comfort. If you were in danger of starvation you would be somewhere else, seeking food. It is more likely than not that you have a place to sleep tonight. You probably have some money in your pockets. You will not die through not reading this book.

Yet few of us live without financial fear. Your job may not be certain, you may have taken on more debt than you would like. You may be reluctant to spend what you have because of nagging uncertainty. There are many very rich people for whom what they have will never be enough that they feel truly secure. Most of us have ancestral voices in our heads – grandparents or parents who lived through the depression, the war or 1950's austerity or who experienced equivalent deprivations somewhere. There are today's specific concerns about recession or worse.

Beyond the specific fears are further realms of disquiet. The money system does not seem as if it is designed to nourish us. Always there seem to be others who want whatever money we have. Governments want tax revenues and utility bills need paying. Shopkeepers want us to buy stuff, and we know that standing behind them are queues of manufacturers who need to keep production lines running and distribution chains with trucks to fill.

One flipside of fear is greed. Closely coupled with the fear that we will lose what we have is the fear that we have not got enough. There is a cavern in the pit of our stomachs that we have to fill, and nothing ever seems to fill it. Of course, this sensation may not only attach to money. We can be greedy for affection or sex, always seeking the next partner, the one who will love us enough to end that emptiness. But greed for money and for the things that money will buy is familiar. If we haven't felt it ourselves, we know people who have.

Our fear of not having enough money and our insecurity about maintaining what we have can both be very disempowering. The feeling that we are not in command, that we are victims of a world ready to sabotage our security can lead to a desire for power. Desire for power is not the same thing as being potent. When we are empowered we feel that we can achieve what we need to achieve. We have power within ourselves. Desire for power looks outside of ourselves. It seeks power over external circumstances in the illusion that this will satisfy our internal craving. It is another chasm that can never be filled.

Fear can also manifest as selfishness. In the midst of feeling that there is not enough, it takes courage to consider the needs of others, and to risk that we will be left wanting. Or it can make us possessive, unable to let go of what we have, even when it is surplus to need. It inhibits our sharing, piles up our unused things in attics and garages "just in case".

These are human fallibilities which most of us have experienced in some measure and which many of us have either worked through, or are able to consciously push ourselves beyond. I may be too ashamed of my selfish thoughts to actually behave as I feel. I may be conscious of my social obligation to buy a round of drinks even when it makes me feel anxious. I may force myself to clear the garage, to take my unwanted things to the charity shop or recycle them through eBay.

If these were merely personal experiences for each of us, perhaps the consequences would be less widespread and maybe not too serious. The view that will be presented in this chapter is that the effects run deep into the culture and have in fact been embedded and systematised. The money system that we have built is predicated on these emotional responses. In many cases it encourages them and feeds off them. The results are unhealthy in the short term and unsustainable in the longer term. They are among the causes of our difficulty in managing the complexities that we referred to in the previous chapter. If we are to find our way out of the current crisis, something new is required.

According to one dictionary I consulted, the word "economics" has Greek roots, relating to *oikos,* which is a house or dwelling and *nomos,* its organising principle. It thus has overtones of stewardship and household management, hence our modern usage where economy means restraint, where we economise in our use of resources. The word "money" is derived from the Latin *monere* which means to cause someone to think, or remember. It is a reminder, like a mnemonic, or sometimes a warning.

If we think of money as a reminder, then the phrase used by economists "growth in the money supply" takes on a new quality. It now means that we have added to our stock of reminders. It asks us perhaps to become mindful, or even conscious. One of the things that we know about emotions is that they can interfere with our thinking. When I am fearful or angry I may not behave logically. Unmanaged emotion goes hand in hand with irrational behaviour. We cease to be mindful. So it was probably not our smartest move to construct our money system on the emotions of greed and fear.

Let's look at how these emotions drive our use of money. With "greed" we have a word rooted in Saxon and Old English meaning hunger. When we are hungry, we want more, which is what we recognise as the defining characteristic of greed. However, when hungry we have the possibility of satisfaction. Greed is never satisfied. Humans possess a positive quality, an impulse towards creation and to self-expression which results in us making things and in a gesture towards others. Greed is a gesture towards ourselves.

At the head of this chapter is a quotation from author John Lahr about society's use of advertising to "drive people crazy with lust". Advertising is a process designed to tell us about the latest and newest thing, and persuade us that we need it. Occasionally it is merely to remind us of a brand name for something that we see as a staple, like the old enamel signs for Pears Soap. Mostly it is to tell us that we need to drink Coke not water, that we really need a new sofa and that HD /3D / BluRay TV is the only way to view. It targets children so that they nag their parents and it is projected at every one of us regardless of our capacity to purchase. And at the same time, the credit cards and loan companies are also advertising, kindly offering to ensure that we can satisfy these lusts.

> *Advertising may be described as the art of arresting human intelligence long enough to get money from it*
>
> *Stephen Leacock*

Growing the greed

There are other driving forces behind the triggering of our greed and lust. Companies need to sell products in order for business to continue. But it is not enough that they can sell 1000 items last year and 1000 items this year. Growth is expected and demanded. Company shareholders may have made 10 cents per share in dividend (the profit that the company distributes to them) last year but will be looking for 12 cents this year. That requires sales growth or cost reduction. The value of their shares, should they wish to sell, also varies according to the amount of dividend income the share might produce. Shareholders want growth.

But we are mostly not talking about individual shareholders. Shareholding is institutionalised. You and I may well depend on share performance for our pensions. We may have put money in unit trusts or managed investments. When we pay insurance premiums, the money that the insurance companies hold in case of claims may also be invested in stocks and shares. They look for profit from capital and not just from the service provision. Your pension fund, your retirement annuity or your endowment mortgage are likely to have been sold to you with an illustration of growth. There may have been promises of 3%, 5%, even 7% per annum returns.

And behind those companies there is a government. Governments also require growth. Regularly, the national economic spokesperson will deliver an economic forecast which will predict the percentage of growth in the economy for the coming year. On those growth assumptions he will base his calculations of how much money will be available through taxes to fund services, to renew infrastructure or to invest in new capital programmes. Some of those expenditures will need to be financed by borrowing. Those who lend the government their money will also expect a return. They don't just want their money back. They want it to grow. Only if the economy grows can the government can fulfil that expectation without taxing you more next year than this.

At every level – that of your credit card repayment, your bank account, personal unit trust, your company or private pension or your stake in our national public assets and government bonds – you are hooked in to the demand for growth. We are all running like crazy just to keep up with our own expectations. We are the donkey pursuing the dangling carrot on a string, the hamster in a wheel, the runners on a treadmill.

How then do we cope with the pressure of expectations that rise every year? The way we do it is to count on an annual pay increase. That drives inflation. That too is now built in to the system, and when times get hard, and employers talk about pay freezes, we are shocked, even outraged. How does an employer find the money to pay their people more? It can get more per head out of them – growing the company with the same workforce, or staying the same size and laying people off. Or it can pass the cost on to others.

Most of us have lived our lives with inflation, and it makes us fearful. Most of us know that it eats away at any gains that we make from our annual increase. At its worst, the inflation generally may be greater than our individual rise, and that is when we get even more fearful, because we may not make ends meet. We may have to cut back. We worry that our pension may be eroded and the law in many countries insists that we are reminded in every advertisement that the value of our investments can go down as well as up. Our fear and our greed are embedded in the system, in continual tension with one another.

Everyone is caught up in this balancing act. It is like being on a bicycle. The only thing that stops us tipping sideways (i.e. falling off) is the forward movement, which allows us to rebalance second by second. And we cycle in huge groups close together. There is only so much individual wobble we can cope with and if one crashes, we may all end up in a heap. So no-one can slow down individually. We either keep pedalling together forever / until exhausted, or we all slow down together and stop. Are you feeling tired yet?

More to the point, are you wondering at all who is in charge? We have become accustomed to thinking that this is a problem for governments, that if they knew what they were doing, they could fix all of this. Perhaps it is becoming apparent to you that they can't. They can tweak the system and adjust the balances, stop us from wobbling too far one side or the other. But they are part of the bicycle race too. They are doing what we ask them to do. In 1992 during the American Presidential Election, successful candidate Bill Clinton made the phrase "It's the economy, stupid" central to his campaign. It is always the economy. So don't expect any politician to tell you that they are not in charge of it. They have to believe that they are, because we demand it of them.

But whether or not they can tell you so, it is the truth. Somehow the system got to be in charge and it got that way because we wanted something from it. As we will see in the next chapter, the banks have made it worse and they have manipulated the system further to suit themselves but they didn't create the problem on their own. Nor are banks the only problem because the system itself creates major irrationality and harm in the way that corporations are owned and governed and in the forces that drive decision-making. We will discuss this in Chapter 8. We will also see that governments don't have our best interests at heart, even when they think they do. Money was invented to serve us, but now we serve it, because we have built this huge rolling road that we ride our bicycles along. We don't even have the option to stop, not unless we can turn off the rolling road!

This condition has now become a factor in our democratic system, according to John Bunzl, founder of the International Simultaneous Policy Organisation and co-author of "Monetary Reform – Making it Happen". He makes the point that the trend of decreasing election turnout is driven in some measure by the way our votes have become irrelevant. Regardless of our polling booth choices, governments will do what they are driven to do by external views of our economic status. This was very visible during the 2010 UK election (and since) when the need to appease the world financial community over our debt management became a driving force to the economic arguments. In 2011 external pressure unseated governments in Greece and Italy.

Our individual disempowerment and fear is mirrored in a collective equivalent. On our behalf, governments too oscillate around fear and greed, attempting to balance the books and maintain a standard of living. Any change they make risks bringing disadvantage if it is seen to make us uncompetitive. Bunzl's Simpol organisation draws the logical conclusion that in order to make change, we will require simultaneous policy co-ordination to take place internationally. (www.simpol.org)

While Simpol is almost certainly correct in its viewpoint, the underlying need is for us to know what changes are required. The system reflects our collective choices to date. What must our new choices be? How do we regain the upper hand, and make money once again into a supportive tool, a system that serves us all?

The bad news is that it is up to us. It is only if we stop wanting what we can't have and possibly don't even need and cease fearing what we might lose, that we can find our way out. The good news is that it is up to us. We have the power to change our mindset and to rebuild the system in such a way that it serves humanity and serves the planet.

Summary Nuggets

We have an emotional relationship with money.

Our view of money and our use of it are affected by fear, greed, desire for power selfishness, possessiveness and desire to control.

These viewpoints and emotions are built in to the construction of our money systems.

4. Money gone mad

A bank is a place that will lend you money if you can prove that you don't need it

This chapter contains a lot of figures and is one of the two most technical sections. There is one part that may even seem incomprehensible and that is just the point. It really doesn't make sense. Even if you don't understand all of it I hope that you will get the gist of how the world has been treating money because it is at the core of what we have to change. The good news is that the world can function very well if it does change.

In chapter 2, we noted that in the transition between stages 4 and 5, money became finally disconnected from the rest of material reality. To repeat what we said there, "Money becomes its own reference point, and the aspiration to link it to physical reality has been broken. This allows the Stage 5 Values system to make money itself into the focus. The creativity which propelled the industrial and technological age to make goods has been diverted into finding ways to make money. Not to make money as an outcome of creating goods and services, but rather to make money by growing the money itself." It is closely connected with the replacement of capital by debt, and the development of a debtist system.

What does that mean? How do you grow money without growing something real? Where is the shift from planting seeds and doing work to raise crops, from using our hands or machine tools to turn raw materials into manufactured goods?

Interest and Usury

The simplest way of growing money is the one we are most familiar with. It is called "interest". Interest is what we call the system whereby I lend you money from my surplus not because I want to help you do something of benefit, not from my care for you, but out of my care for my money. I am not interested in you. I am interested in my money.

It is this simple distinction in relationship which caused the Judaic, Christian and Islamic religions all to define such a transaction as "usury". That means what it appears to mean, which is that we use one another. It's not nice. Nowadays it would mean charging unfair and excessive amounts of interest, like pay-day loans but originally it meant charging any interest at all. Of course it is several centuries since those religions began to water down their prohibition. Islam has held on more strongly but interest is the way of the world.

You may be able to see that a moderate degree of interest is now simply built in to the systems that were described in Chapter 3. Because everyone does it, at low levels it is self-cancelling. The interest you earn may do no more than keep pace with inflation. It merely protects people from losing out when they lend to someone else. But most people expect to make more than that. Sometimes the justification for a lender is that they have taken a risk. Investing in someone else to help them start a business is a gesture that may not pay off. Interest is the reward for taking that risk, and the compensation for the times when the investment is unsuccessful.

There are some very sophisticated versions of the logic and they can give the impression that interest is a good thing, that it is fair and natural, that it is simply a way to encourage people to use their surplus to support others, or to take care of what we ourselves have put by "for a rainy day" – our protection against the time when our crops are washed out. It is very persuasive and we have become used to it. To see its drawbacks we need to look at what would have happened in a moneyless world, or if interest was still legally prohibited.

So imagine that you have a surplus – whether it be corn, goats or pottery. Within the limits of perishability you can store it. Since it is not money you can sell it. You can barter it for something else. You can lend it to someone. Or you can give it away. As with our earlier non-monetary transactions, these options are direct, and allow limited opportunity to (ab)use the other party. None of them have serious "karmic" downsides. If what goes around comes around, you'll be OK.

When this surplus is represented in money, but interest is still not allowed, you still have the "store, lend and give" options. Of those three only the "lend" option carries an element of risk, and you have not done damage that warrants comeback against you. You cannot use or abuse another. All of these decisions can be made in a personal balance where you place your care for your own needs on one side of the scale and your care for your fellow humans on the other. There may be elements of kudos and satisfaction to include in the balance and perhaps the value of knowing that someone owes you a favour or that you are repaying one. But whatever those criteria, they are personal and at the root they are about care for human values. Even if money is involved it is probably not the only consideration. And whatever happens, you are personally responsible for it.

In the event that you have a very substantial surplus and are more than adequately protected against contingencies then there is an additional consideration. With goods, or money in an interest-free system you cannot make more by holding on to it. Beyond a certain point, excess has no value. At best, goods may be stored in anticipation of a price rise, or in case of future shortage. To get something for your money you have to spend it. Soccer genius George Best experienced the value of vast excesses of money, saying *"I spent a lot of money on booze, birds and fast cars. The rest I just squandered."* In the absence of interest, if you want to make more money you have to make it work for you. This provides an incentive to keep the excess in circulation. Later on we will look at why this is a good thing, even why it might be seen as essential to our future.

So while there may be some good reasons for allowing interest, it is not as benign a mechanism as it might seem, and its limitations should be taken into account in constructing a balanced money system. Most of all, we must guard against the idea that we can simply "grow" money. Let us now pursue what trouble that idea gets us into, examine the outcome when money-culture meets greed. This story has two parts which will be familiar to all – the rise in house prices and the recent financial crisis. What is still less well understood is how these two came to be linked, and how the problems continue to threaten us.

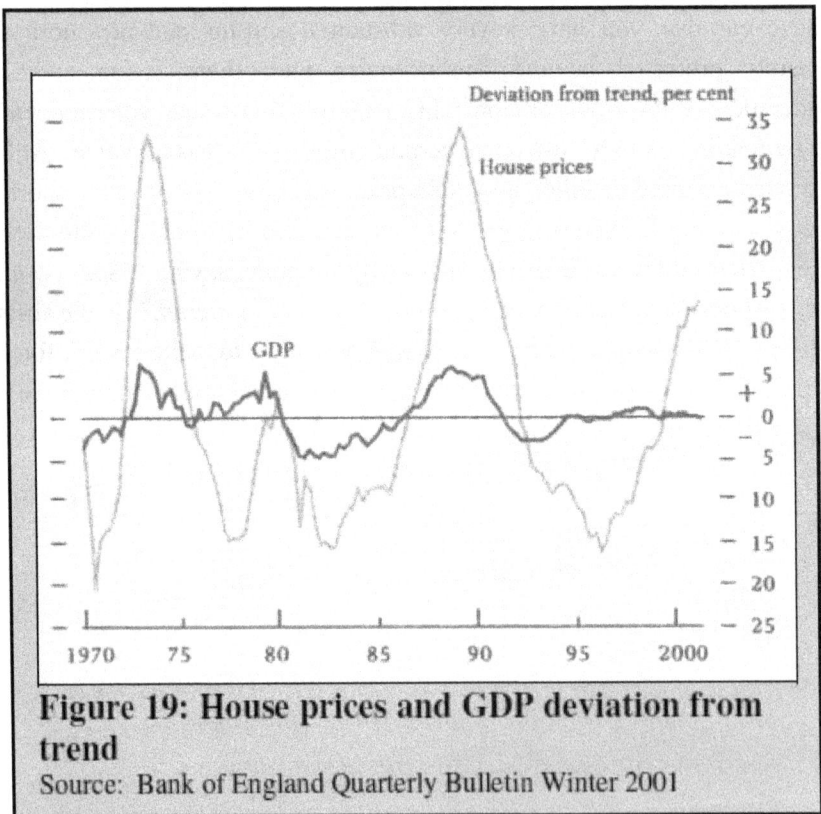

Figure 19: House prices and GDP deviation from trend
Source: Bank of England Quarterly Bulletin Winter 2001

How the world came to an end - almost

Over the past 50 years, house values have risen by an average of 2.7% each year. The average rise in real earnings over that period was 2%. There was generally some value in investing money in a house. But the 2.7% increase has not been steady. There have been times of rise and fall. There have been four distinct periods of rapid real house-price growth: 1971–73, 1977–80, 1985–89 and 1998–2007 (See graph below). Each of these periods was followed by a significant fall in real house prices. Typically, to see an assured profit from property investment requires 10 to 15 years.

Like all investment cycles, timing is everything. You can make money in the stock market if you buy stocks when they are cheap and sell when they are expensive. Get it the wrong way round and you lose money. Housing is no different. The latest of those four rapid growth cycles started in 1998. In the 8 years 1999 to 2007 the average increase was approximately 10% per year. A house worth £100K at the start of that cycle would sell for £260K at the end.

The UK is just a typical example. According to estimates by The Economist, the total value of residential property in developed economies rose by more than $30 trillion over the years 2000-2005, to over $70 trillion, an increase equivalent to 100% of those countries' combined Gross Domestic Products. Not only does this dwarf any previous house-price boom, it is larger than the global stockmarket bubble in the late 1990s (an increase over five years of 80% of GDP) or America's stockmarket bubble in the late 1920s (55% of GDP). In other words, it was the biggest bubble in history. But where stock bubbles largely affect investors, housing affects almost all of us.

During this time, the financial world lost its marbles. Granted this was the longest boom cycle in 50 years, but there was nothing to guarantee it would last forever. Booms never do, but we started to behave as if it would. Individually people were buying and selling in order to bank the gains on a 3-bed semi so as to use the same level of mortgage to finance a 4-bed detached. In spite of estate agent and tax costs (stamp duty) it seemed to make financial sense, because the new property would be ours for life. So more and more people were buying, creating exactly the demand-exceeds-supply conditions that drive up prices. It was self-fulfilling behaviour.

Now think about how people were paying for these purchases. Most of them had mortgages. When a mortgage lender puts up the money for a purchase, it takes a risk. Can you pay the money back, it would ask? It would expect you to prove it, too. In earlier decades that risk was managed by two simple mechanisms. Firstly, you had to have saved or been given at least 10% of the price of the house to put down as a deposit. The bank would secure its lending on the remaining 90%. Secondly you would have to show your ability to pay back by proving your earnings ability. In 1978, when I first bought a house, I could only borrow an amount three times my annual salary. That was normal.

During this last boom, lenders got cocky. Becoming over-confident that prices would rise forever, they took a different view of risk. If prices were rising, then it didn't matter so much if a few people failed to pay. Lenders could foreclose and still make money on the rising value of the house. If in doubt they could get the borrower – you and me - to take out an insurance against default. So the insurance companies were also involved, making money off protection policies. On that basis, lenders would not only give you 100% of the property price – no deposit required – they would give you extra to furnish and move in. And they would offer up to four times annual earnings. Possibly they would not check at all. You could self-certify your ability to pay. Who cared? Values would go up for ever and everyone would be in profit.

> *Accountants are the witch-doctors of the modern world and willing to turn their hands to any kind of magic.*
>
> *Lord Justice Harman*

We all know now that it simply couldn't work, and we have all watched the value of our properties fall back. We have seen too, that the consequence for lenders is that they became over-exposed to risk. They couldn't afford to lend any more money. And that is what a credit crunch is. There is no more money in the system to lend, because collectively more is owed than we can be confident of seeing paid back. Banks were in crisis and had to be bailed out by governments. You may wish to lodge a question in the back of your mind –

where did that bail-out money come from? Perhaps you know the answer. But we will come back to it shortly.

For now, we should follow the thread of over-lending, protection insurances and moneyculture because we haven't yet reached the point of genuine "mad scientist"[ii] inventiveness in how many of the world's financial institutions thought they could make money grow by itself.

Our story continues to be underpinned by greed and fear. As individuals, many of us were caught up in this bubble and excited by the prospect of making money without having to work for it. Others of us were fearful that we would miss out, or be left behind, unable to buy a house at all. Parents were cajoled, possibly putting up their own properties as additional security. Nobody wanted to miss out on this free lunch. The financial institutions did not want to miss out on it either, but for their lunch they wanted caviar and champagne. They got their boffins to come up with ways to cash in. They took the greed and made into a system.

So let's see if we can get our heads around how they did this. Actually, it's really just an extension of what we did individually. One of the barriers to understanding may be that it looks too stupid to be true. But it is true.

> *Nothing is illegal if one hundred well-placed businessmen decide to do it*
>
> *Andrew Young*

[ii]   I am indebted to Centre for Human Emergence colleague Said Dawlabani, author of the groundbreaking book "Memenomics" for the "mad scientist" imagery and for much of the original research behind this chapter. The biblical parodies below are my responsibility.

The Set-up

Financial institutions make money by moving money around. All the money is on paper. Somebody wants to borrow money and someone wants to lend it. Someone else wants to invest money safely and get a good return. The pieces of paper that do this are like loan agreements and mortgages, but bigger. Loans are secured on a promise to pay and mortgages secured on the property value. These bigger pieces of paper have names like Bonds and Gilts, depending on who is lending, who is borrowing and what the security is. Gilts are government bonds, so named because they were once backed by gold. The big pieces of paper are sold by brokers who make a commission – just like the person who sells you your car insurance. But the numbers are much bigger.

Like all commission-driven sales processes, the ease of your sale is helped if your product looks really good. So the institutions looked at how to make a really impressive product out of the housing bubble. Instead of an insurance company investing $100M in Microsoft shares or letting some government borrow it at interest, what if other institution would sell them a slice of the housing bubble? They could take the little individual pieces of paper (mortgage debt) that housing lenders have, bundle them up and sell them on. The purchase price (less commission) flows back to the lenders, giving them more money to lend. Remember that in this scenario it is believed that property prices will never fall again. They "know" the bundles are secure because there is guaranteed growth, so investors will want them. One day, investors will want some interest, but these will be funded by the instalments from mortgage-holders. Hardly any of those will default (rising house prices, strong economy) so there will be no problem. "And we shall call these bundles of paper "Collateralised Debt Obligations" and we shall produce brilliant mathematical equations which show how they are guaranteed to make money."

So that is what happened[iii]. These kinds of products are called "derivatives" because they are investments that are derived from other transactions, as well as

---

[iii] "The Big Short" by Michael Lewis tells this story well.

possibly for mathematical reasons. They are further from "real stuff" and they exist only on paper. Now you might wonder why no-one saw the flaw in this process (and very few people did). That is because there was a theoretical back-stop against anyone who challenged the risk. The regulatory system for financial markets is in place to monitor schemes like this and to protect the public against frauds and scams. These are the people who in theory to have the expertise to recognise such weaknesses. Unfortunately they didn't so this mechanism failed, leaving those less expert with a false sense of confidence.

There are credit rating agencies whose function it is to assess any potential debtor. You probably know that these exist for individuals, and that if your personal credit rating is damaged by defaulting on a loan, you may struggle to get your credit limit raised when you next apply. This too happens at the highest level, and the specialist agencies assess countries, corporations and major products like derivatives. Greece was in the news because its credit rating was down the tubes after the crunch, requiring the rest of Europe to put up security to keep it in business. Ireland suffered similarly and Italy and Spain were both under threat. Everyone at every level gets credit-assessed. The European currency is in jeopardy and might easily have broken up or broken down. Even in 2014 it was fragile with France and Italy asking to have their borrowing limits raised and in 2015 Greece's problems with debt threatened the whole Euro system.

The Credit rating agencies assessed the collateralised debt obligations (CDO's) and stamped them all with the most excellent triple-A ratings. They fell for the clever equations and didn't see the underlying problem. The emperor's clothes were absolutely beautiful. Of course you might question how hard they looked. The whole industry is a revolving door, with regulators and government advisers recruited from financial institutions and all of them subject to the same group-think. The head of the US Federal Reserve, Alan Greenspan, whose credibility at the time approached divine status, also saw that they were good. And behold it was very good, so we entered the fantasy garden of Eden, where banks, insurance companies, investment companies and pension fund managers all over the world would buy these packages of derivatives and sell them to each other.

No-one knew what the underlying debts were. It is doubtful even now that they are known.

Just for completeness, be aware that the same failures of risk management that we described for individual housing were also applying to major developments. Where once, the construction of a shopping centre (mall) would have required the developer to put up 30% of the funding and to show that many of the retail units were pre-contracted for occupancy, these criteria were also weakened. Lots of brokers made lots of commission and no-one wanted or was able to stop any of it. Commercial property development was just as vulnerable as domestic housing, with more zeroes.

The knock-down

Eventually the music stopped and the dancers came off the dance floor. Some of the people who had been sold unsafe mortgages began to default. The house of cards became shaky and eventually collapsed. One token institution (Lehman Brothers) was allowed to go out of business. Iceland went bankrupt and defaulted on its debts. The UK government persuaded Lloyds Bank to buy HBOS. Government money was pumped into RBS in the UK and into the big federal mortgage lenders known as Freddie Mac and Fannie Mae in the USA[iv]. Bailouts also went to General Motors and others. Trillions of dollars were printed by governments to throw after the trillions of dollars that had disappeared. Printing money is frowned on by economists because it creates inflation, so a new label was invented. They called it "Quantitative Easing". At the same time approximately 3.4 trillion dollars was written off according to IMF estimates in late 2009.

Note that the estimates for the size of write-downs fluctuate according to the current value of the stockmarket. At one time there were estimates above $17 trillion. It has since come down but a further dip could take the figure up again.

[iv] This story is told by Andrew Ross Sorkin in "Too big to fail" and in the 2011 movie that followed

Be aware also that the figures for potential losses in areas like CDO's may be viewed by individual companies as covered by their insurance. They see their small picture as rosy, ignoring the fact that if many companies were to make simultaneous claims this too could precipitate domino-like collapse. The insurance money comes from somewhere – other bank loans, pension fund stakeholders and even the premiums on our other policies.

In the bailout process it is crucial to recognise that nothing has been created except money; the new money does not represent anything in the real world. There are no new goods to buy with it. All that can happen is that the money which was previously there is now worth less than before. There is more money and less that you can buy. And where some money was written off – recognised as unrecoverable bad debt - that money has come out of someone's pocket somewhere. Out of your pension fund maybe. The new money does not come back to you. The total in the US has reached approximately $2.5 <u>Trillion</u> and the equivalent in the UK is £375 Billion ($600 Bn).

And so finally we are in the biggest "funny money" game of all. In order to deliver these huge bail-outs, governments have to get money from somewhere. So they borrow it. Governments don't have any money of their own. They just have yours and mine. The income that they expect to have, in order to promise payback, comes from our taxes. In the UK we are approaching the 2015 election where leaders are talking about deficits and spending cuts just as they did in 2010. Deficit is the word for taking out a mortgage on GB Ltd. Our household income and expenditure do not balance. Now our money has to go to paying off the debt.

But the thing that we should be really scared about is that all that borrowing did not fix the underlying problem. The banks had run out of money to lend and giving them some more was meant to get the economy going again. But much of the money went into building up reserves to protect banks from the risks that they had run before but now have to treat more seriously. As a result not much came back out into the economy. The hole was too big to fill. And what money there is, they were reluctant to lend, since the subsequent recession meant businesses were perceived to be more at risk. The banks say they want to lend money, but only those who don't need it should apply. Those businesses that have done well are sitting on their cash piles too.

The bicycle we have been riding had a hole in its tyre. The government has been pumping the tyre up, borrowing money from our future. But there's no more money to be borrowed and the tyres are going down. The bicycles will get harder to pedal and more wobbly.

The aftermath

It is very hard to know how big the problem is, because many figures are hidden inside complex financial packages that no-one can unravel. Some websites copy each other's figures without providing backup. It is also very difficult to get a sense of scale. The debt figures I am about to quote are mostly from "official" sources and are high by today's standards. At the same time they are relatively lower than after WWII when the costs of war had to be repaid, but then times were extremely hard for the next decade.

Having said all that, I suggest that the figures that follow are cause for considerable concern

- U.S. Federal Budget Deficit Bomb. Federal debt almost doubled by 2010 to $14.3 trillion vs. $7.8 trillion in 2005 and reached $16.5 trillion by mid-2013. The annual deficit in 2013 was $0.69 trillion (690 billion) and the Congressional Budget Office predicts continued growth to 2020 by which time it will total of almost 100% of GDP. By way of comparison, the annual deficit in the UK is $177 Billion, whereas Germany has a surplus of $266 Billion

- The Chinese national domestic debt now totals $23 trillion. The British National Debt is around £1.4 trillion ($2 trillion) which equates to 90% of GDP.

- Consumer-debt Bomb. Household debt is similar in many countries with the total (mortgages, car finance, credit cards and bank loans etc.) adding up to percentages of household income such as 84% in the USA and ranging from 170% to 220% of income in several European countries. In the UK we are believed to have a trillion dollars on our credit cards alone. That is over £15,000 for every British man, woman and child.

- In the UK, government net borrowing (according to the Office of National Statistics) was 6.5% of GDP in 2012. This is £105 Billion and is less than previous years and forecast to decline to zero by 2018-19. That is if you believe that such a target is achievable – which would largely fly in the face of history.

- Much of countries' debts can be internal, from one institution to another. However one-third of US debt is owed to other countries, with China notably holding 8% and Japan 7% of it.

- Global Real Estate Bomb. There continues to be a Real Estate bubble, with developments standing empty and notably some whole cities in China built but not populated. In the UK, France, Netherlands, Sweden and several other countries, house-price to income ratios are well above normal trend levels. The result is that warnings abound of another property price bubble. Economist Nouriel Roubini (Guardian, Dec 2013) has said *"What we are witnessing in many countries looks like a slow-motion replay of the last housing market train wreck"*.

- Social Security and medical care Bomb. Aging populations need increasing pension and healthcare support at a time of financial stress. In America, the government is hugely in debt to itself in these areas. The prescription drugs bill alone in the USA is estimated above $35 trillion

- Bailout Bombs. Tax credits, loans, cash and purchase of toxic assets from Wall Street banks were estimated at $23.7 trillion. In the UK there are still banks effectively in public ownership, awaiting the time when shares owned by the government might find buyers in the market.

But the biggest of all is the Derivatives Bomb. According to the 2013 report from the U.S. Comptroller of the Currency's office the total notional amount of derivatives held by U.S. commercial banks and savings associations, as of 12/31/12, was a staggering $223 trillion. The four largest U.S. banks shown

53

above hold 93% of these contracts. To put these overwhelming numbers into perspective, the U.S. economy only generates about $15.5 trillion in gross national product per annum; so, we're talking over 14 years' worth of GNP tied up in notional derivatives exposure, with the four main banks soaking up over 13 years' worth of the total. In terms of product type, 80% of the total notional derivatives exposure is in interest rate swap contracts.

The USA appears to be typical. The total annual GDP (the monetary value of everything that we do) from all nations is around $50 trillion. The estimated value of all derivatives is estimated by some as **$1 quadrillion** ($1000 trillion)[v]. That is rather like you and me owing the next 10-15 years of our household income, which we might look upon as the defining sign of bankruptcy. Who's doing the global audit? And how do all these figures compare with the mere 2 trillion dollars that were written down during the last crash?

The problems don't stop there. Not only is the bulk of the market private and hard to track, but it still isn't properly regulated. In the USA the Volcker Rule limits in theory the speculative trading that commercial banks can do but it is much less rigorous than actual separation of commercial lending and investment banking that existed under the Glass-Steagall regulatory framework that was in place from 1933 until the Reagan era. This lack of separation combined with the inscrutability of computer-based trading and spurious investment vehicles to create the almost perfect storm of 2008-9.

While that amount might be far less than the $1 quadrillion, which could be good news, it is outweighed by the bad news. It is hard to know because when banks trade these instruments they frequently pass them off to others and so the figure is very hard to compute due to what's known as counterparty risk. If you buy a stock for cash, you can't lose more than you invest. But if you sell $1,000 of derivatives and collateralize it by purchasing $900 of another offsetting derivative, how much are you really at risk? In theory, you can only lose $100.

---

[v]   http://business.time.com/2013/03/27/why-derivatives-may-be-the-biggest-risk-for-the-global-economy/

But if the person from whom you purchased the $900 derivative ends up defaulting, then you're on the hook for all $1,000 you sold. So are you at risk for $100 or $1,000? It's hard to know. Regulators try to assign weights and probabilities to determine capital requirements. But the bottom line is simple: if the whole market comes apart, everyone is at risk for a lot more than they expect and no-one knows the true amount. Thus the bad news is that no-one knows how much debt is out there. I am told that one bank asked by the then head of the UK Financial Services Authority to provide a figure for its position took six months to get an answer. This is part of the reason for such high levels of fear.

In our list above we referred to some of the areas of "sovereign debt" – money owed by countries. We need to look at just how much of a concern this can be. As an example, Italian debt (from the Italian government's own figures) amounts to around 2.3 Trillion Euros and ticks higher at the rate of 3000 Euros per second. This is 136% of their annual income (GDP).[vi]

When a new instalment is due to service that debt, it could come from their economic surplus, only there isn't one. That means they must borrow. So they borrow on today's credit card (Bond market) to pay off yesterday. But because they are now more risky, today's bond is more expensive. Even if the government cuts spending, they have no prospect of paying this off. After several years of pressure it was agreed that the European Central Bank should act as "lender of last resort" in order to secure the position. But the ECB only has the money which other European countries choose to give it out of their surpluses, unless it issues more money, which reduces the value of the money in all other Euro countries. In order to make this scenario palatable, the agreement being called for is for a cross-Eurozone agreement on tight budgets. Unfortunately this would only stop the problem from getting worse. It doesn't solve it; the bottom-line truth is that there is no realistic possibility of Italy, the fourth largest economy in the EU, paying off the 2.3 trillion. More unfortunately France, the third largest, is now seeking looser criteria. Britain, the second largest, is not in a position to bail out anyone which leaves Germany holding the

---

[vi] You can view most nations at www.nationaldebtclocks.org

baby. President Nixon's attitude to Italy was "Well, I don't give a shit about the lira." Globalism means that his successors have to think differently.

Almost all nations have such debts – even Germany's is at 80% of GDP. Many banks are holding the bonds which are at risk. Those banks are covering the risk by insuring the debt with insurance companies that could not conceivably pay in the event of default. So it looks alright on paper but is built on vapour. The insurance company shares which are at risk in the event of default are owned by banks, other insurance companies and your pension fund. They all own each other's shares. Everybody holds a piece of each other's paper money, banks and countries alike. This appears to be a spread risk, but the truth beneath is that it makes the risk invisible and establishes an all-or-none scenario. If one bank or one country goes it is likely to take the rest with it.

Two weeks before the Royal Bank of Scotland failed and had to be bailed out by the UK government, its then Chief Executive Sir Fred Goodwin was on camera saying that the amount of derivatives owned by the bank was minuscule and represented totally insignificant levels of risk. Two weeks later the declared amount of default was £4Billion and this was not the whole of the bank's exposure. This incompetence did not prevent Sir Fred receiving severance compensation of about £150Million. Nor has it changed anything about the level of transparency. Nor has it truly changed the amount of paper debt, whether labelled as Derivatives, Bonds, Insurances or whatever. Now as then, we are deeply in debt, and no-one has a way out.

So now we know. This is what happens to a society driven by fear and greed, a society that is living in the fantasy of free lunches, a society where the system allowed the idea to develop that we could grow money, a society where we are leaning forward further than our legs can keep up with. This is a world where our interest in money finally went completely over the edge and lost all relationship to the real world or to each other. The money system is broken. Governments and institutions don't want to admit it because they don't have an alternative. We will see later the specific part played by banking institutions' self-interest. Most of our elected officials and their paid advisers don't understand the problem and still think that the financial sector delivers

56

economic benefit. We will see that largely it doesn't. Plan A is bankrupt. You might want to start asking them "what is Plan B"? You might want to look at ours in our closing chapters.

But don't be too worried. Stay conscious through all of this – conscious of the imaginary exercise that you went through in the introduction. It is only the money that is broken. The world tomorrow will still be as the world today. The sun will shine and the flowers will bloom. It is merely the money that has to be fixed. That just requires us to think differently, so the way we think is our next topic.

Summary Nuggets

The desire to make money grow by itself independent of any real creation of goods and services began with interest.

It developed into systems of complex debt and sophisticated paper instruments.

The failure to understand complex instruments, together with greed and naive over-confidence led to the debt crisis.

National economies also function on very high levels of indebtedness. We replaced the capitalist system with the debtist system.

Because we measure success via money there is a conventional belief that an economy grows simply because the numbers get bigger. This causes governments to believe that the finance institutions are contributing to the economy.

Section 2: New ways of thinking about money?

"There is no better way to get people to do your will than to persuade them that there is no alternative, that yours is the only conceivable form of truth."...."In today's market economy, science and business have leagued together to impose a single model of reality, to privatise it through the intellectual property system and to draw profit from it"

"A Peaceable Economy"   Edouard Dommen

5.   Thinking afresh

The desire to hold money as a store of wealth is a barometer of the degree of our distrust of our own calculations and conventions concerning the future….It operates, so to speak, at a deeper level of our motivation.

John Maynard Keynes

For the avoidance of any doubt whatsoever this isn't about economics, not as we know it. What has just been described should make it quite clear that we don't get out of this mess only by tweaking interest rates and regulating the money supply. That is a "deck-chairs on the Titanic" mentality. This is a problem that cannot be solved from the same level of thinking as that which created it. This is a problem that is solved by shifting to a new level of thinking and recognising the deeper levels of motivation in human nature.

That new thinking cannot happen only at the systems level. The fix does not come just by changing the way that banks and insurance companies function, although that will help and is an essential step. It does not come just because we alter the tax system. In the end, while banks and governments may seem to have their own agendas, they operate in the field that we create around them. If we want banks to offer us a free lunch then they will respond. They will take their own bite out first, of course. If we vote for politicians because they offer easy solutions rather than facing underlying problems, they will tend in that direction. Bankers and politicians are not that different from the rest of us in how they think. They are just more often successful at making money from it.

So if we want things to change we cannot afford to be passive. We cannot wait for the current leaders to offer us solutions. They got where they are by doing what was right yesterday. With a few exceptions the potential new leaders are outside the system. Those exceptions will be the ones who spotted the failings and spoke out. They are more likely to be capable of formulating solutions, but we will have to call for them to be recognised. Note that if they don't offer any solutions then they are likely to be destructive and are not the new leaders.

> *Destroying what you don't want is not the same as creating what you do want.*
>
> *Dr. Don E. Beck*

The old system was built on a systemisation of fear, greed, selfishness, possessiveness and desire for power. While some individuals have benefitted much more than others, those mind-sets and emotions are in us. The system is a reflection of our thoughts and desires. We made the choices that constructed the system. If we want a new system we will have to make fresh choices. To make those choices we will have to deal with the emotions that bent our thinking out of shape. The change has to come from us. Once again, the fault lies not in our stars, but in ourselves.

The planet is already bankrupt. As described at the close of the last chapter, we already owe several years of our time and effort. Because we owe those years to each other, and because every increase in borrowing adds a month or a year to the figure, no-one has called in the debt. Yet. But it lurks in the system, waiting to happen. At the time of writing, governments are ceasing to pump up the tyres but it is the only remaining tool in the box. Greece narrowly avoided being the first to go repeating the trick in 2015 and still not off the hook. Italy is both too big to save and too big to fail. Sooner or later the dominoes will start to fall and this paragraph will be redundant.

The con-trick in your spam-box

If your spam box is like mine, you get offers every day of inheritances that are not yours or Nigerian government money that you could have a piece of if you help someone siphon it out of the country. These e-mails persist because there are people who are willing to fall for the con, greedy enough to consider bending the rules. I have never fallen for anything like that, but I have certainly fallen for promises that were too good to be true. I only did so because I too, wanted something for nothing. All con men know this is the reason their scams succeed; the victim wants it to be true. Those spam messages will stop when there is no-one greedy enough to respond to them.

The money system as a whole is a bigger version of our spam box. It offers us free lunches and fantasies of effortless prosperity in property bubbles. It has taken some simple and pragmatic principles and bent them out of their original purpose. It can be argued that when President Nixon ended the gold standard this was a necessity, because the system was too restricted, too clumsy. The complexity that we had to manage was beyond that which could be accomplished. The gold weighed it down, like a racehorse running under handicapping. In the emerging digital world, moving gold bars from vault to vault would not get the job done. In a world which was increasing its resource base at a huge rate, sucking millions of gallons of oil from the Earth and building new goods on an industrial scale, it no longer seemed viable to be anchored to one scarce mineral. When populations are growing exponentially the system has to have some elasticity. Reality was changing, and money needed to find a new way to reflect that. This story about Gold is not entirely true and solutions would have been possible. They still are, as will be discussed later.

Even if that story is accepted there are balances that must be struck and if we needed to lose the specific anchor, it did not serve us that we became completely ungrounded and untethered. We did not replace the Gold mechanism with another which would meet future needs. Those familiar with economic history may recognise that the Bretton Woods agreement after World War 2 rejected Keynes' proposal of a global currency – supported at the time by Britain and vetoed outright by the USA. We may well have proved Keynes right; a global currency might well have reduced much of the instability that we have experienced. It might have fared better than the Euro. Whether that is true is a question for academics. But for the future we will have to be able to manage the complexity if we do not want to give up the benefits of the modern world and we will need an agile money system. That flexibility must be constrained by judgement and common sense. Common sense does not look for free lunches. Common sense does not expect money to grow by itself. It doesn't move from a monetary policy to a money-tree system.

Another aspect of our human frailty is to want something that we cannot have. Every parent knows this. Most children will keep asking for sweets until we say "no". They will want that new XBox today and not to have to wait until Christmas. I love to hear all of the music and have hankerings for hi-fi equipment that I cannot afford right now. It takes an effort of will not to borrow money. I have to learn to be happy today. When we borrow it seems that we borrow from someone else. The reality is that we borrow from our future selves. With greed and desire we no longer stand upright. We move our balance into the future.

To walk, you must lean forward – put your weight ahead of your feet. You then move your feet to get ahead of that movement so as not to fall over. Running is similar, with faster moving feet and a bigger lean-forward. Lean too far and you are flat on your face. In money terms the world has leant too far and has stumbled a little but it is due to fall on its face. We must all learn how to live much closer to present time. We have to find the internal parent within ourselves, the one who says "no" to unhealthy or unrealistic desires.

Imagination is one of the greatest and most defining of human attributes. It is where we enter the realms of the Divine, that we can create reality with our thought. Imagination is unlimited. Physical reality, as far as we have manifested it to date, is not. In the 1960's playwright David Mercer wrote a play titled, "Morgan, a suitable case for treatment". In it, Morgan says "the trouble with reality is that it never lives up to my best fantasies". We are a world of Morgans who have been encouraged to live in fantasy. We are nearly all in need of treatment.

Competition, collaboration and the fear of scarcity

So far I have avoided talking in depth about one of the most fundamental of human fears, and the way that it plays out in our thinking and our money system.

This is the fear of scarcity, that there will not be enough. At one level it is a fear based in reality. Many of us have had real experience at some level of not having enough, for myriad reasons from mother's breast-milk drying up to school bullies who stole our packed lunch. You may even have grown up with deprivation. Many of us have played it out in our money life, missing credit card payments, having loans or mortgages foreclosed. Many more of us have come uncomfortably close to those experiences and we were also brought up by others whose conversation or behaviour reflected historical times of scarcity.

At the same time, most of us in the Western world do not experience true scarcity. We probably have not come close to starvation and death. Far from it. If we carry fears of that kind they are probably not a reflection of our daily experience. Like the fantasies of plenty they are more in our imagination than in reality.

Nevertheless the notion of scarcity is strongly embedded in our cultural mindset. It may initially seem as if we are moving away from the subject of money, but the thought systems and emotions we are about to discuss lie deep within our economic assumptions. We would do well to understand some of what lies beneath that culture. This calls for us to unpick 200 years of intellectual history.

Thomas Malthus was a political economist and demographer, which means that he studied birth and death rates and the factors that influence these. In his 1798 book "an essay on the principle of population" he made the following basic observation, stating that *"Population, when unchecked, increases in a geometrical ratio, Subsistence, increases only in an arithmetical ratio."* That is to say, biological organisms are capable of breeding very fast. A pair of mice, with a gestation period of 21 days and a litter size of 5, given adequate food and absence of predators could produce 2000 offspring in a year. Most animals, including humans, will grow their population exponentially, if unchecked. Food supplies typically do not grow in the same way. As a result, food supply inevitably becomes a constraint on population growth at some point.

Correct though this undoubtedly is, it oversimplifies the natural world. There are many things which operate against the simple Malthusian equation.

1) There are many food sources on the planet. Many of the vegetable sources have been growing for a billion years before animal life came along. We started with a surplus.

2) There are many types of creature on the planet, exploiting multiple food sources. Some of those creatures include other creatures among their food source options – for instance birds which may eat both insects and seeds.

3) It is not only that large creatures feed on the small. For example there are worms that live on animal waste products and maggots which feed on decaying flesh, such that everything is part of a complex cycle where natural systems become ever more complex, with more and more parts to the food chain. Bacteria, the smallest creatures, have huge impact.

4) Our human food-production techniques enable us to grow more than the Earth would produce naturally and to exploit areas which were previously low-yielding.

5) While there may be limits to specific sources of food energy, the planet has energy sources which are continuously replenished. The sun shines day after day and the motions of the Earth and Moon produce tides and wind energy. The Earth itself has heat inside it which continues to produce new land and sources of minerals. Bacteria and algae are also part of the food chain, growing exponentially and adding to the sources of life and nourishment.

A glance at Malthus' wiki quotes page would be sufficient to convince most people that he was a rather depressive individual, who took his basic theory to justify some really quite dubious conclusions about humanity. For example:-

"The labouring poor, to use a vulgar expression, seem always to live from hand to mouth. Their present wants employ their whole attention, and they seldom think of the future. Even when they have an opportunity of saving they seldom exercise it, but all that is beyond their present necessities goes, generally speaking, to the ale house."

But Malthus was a typical product of his times and his class, and was without question influential. Among the people he influenced were Charles Darwin and the generations that read his book. Even the fact that Malthus was writing 10 years before Darwin was born, and 60 years before "On the Origin of Species" was published is in some degree an excuse for his view of nature.

Darwin was quite explicit in his acknowledgement of Malthus' influence, writing in the introduction to that book

"Nothing is easier than to admit the truth of the universal struggle for life, or more difficult than to constantly bear that conclusion in mind. Yet unless it be thoroughly engrained in the mind I am convinced that the whole economy of nature, with every fact on distribution, rarity, abundance, extinction and variation, will be dimly seen or quite misunderstood."

and later

"It is the doctrine of Malthus applied with manifold force to the whole animal and vegetable kingdoms".

Both Malthus and Darwin viewed life- "the economy of nature" - as a struggle, and it is easy to see it as that. People are born and people die, and animals eat each other. They are in a strong tradition of British thought, since 200 years before, philosopher Thomas Hobbes had concluded that human life, if not checked by law and government, would be "solitary, poor, nasty, brutish and short". But it is time to challenge this deep tradition, which misses some fundamental truths about life.

Darwin's viewpoint came to be encapsulated in a phrase which he did not invent, namely "survival of the fittest". Although he appears to have accepted it, it does not do him justice and it has been taken to extremes which are not justified by what he wrote. Darwin's work understood a fundamental truth, which is that organisms change over time in response to environmental conditions. Finches, for instance, evolved into distinct species as their beaks changed shape so that they were better able to eat particular food sources. They became better fitted to their environment and thus they survived.

While it is true that there is an underlying competition for limited resources this is not some kind of simple warfare. And while evolution involves the truth that some live to breed and others die, they are mostly not actively killing each other. The result of evolution was not that one finch reigned supreme, but that a richness of finches developed and co-exist in the Galapagos space. And even where species do kill each other, our usual view of "survival of the fittest" is really quite mistaken. The lioness does not hunt down the strongest antelope in a proof of superiority. She culls the weak and infirm such that the system enhances the fitness of both lions and antelopes.

From Competition to Collaboration

We may appear to have strayed far from the theme of money but this difference in thinking is quite crucial. The competitive view of evolution has led quite explicitly to economic theories about how corporations should behave and it has perpetuated the grim misery of Hobbes and Malthus, in their view that life can **only** be a struggle. When you start with this mindset, you construct systems based on **fear** of one another. You build in competition and under-estimate the value of collaboration. That is what we have done.

Returning to our Spiral Dynamics view of the world, we might see that there are stages where competition and fear is stronger. The power struggle of stage 3 and the competitive achievement dynamics of stage 5 do represent that side of the balance. But they are not the whole story. The ordering principles of stage 4 and the human values of stage 6 both go in the opposite direction.

We are at the stage in our development where we are encountering the limitations of Stage 6. The state of our social evolution as we seek the integration of the next stages demands flexibility and balance. We have to work with one another and we have to work with the planet. This is the basis from which the new money systems will have to be built.

A few billion years ago you would have found very little life on this planet; algae, bacteria, and single-celled organisms would be the full catalogue. It is in the nature of life to develop, and the planet we now inhabit is richly filled with many kingdoms containing great diversity of species. Left to themselves and not messed about with by one over-developed two-legged creature and its technology, those species and kingdoms would continue to interact, adapt, self-balance in relation to one another and in relation to climate cycles, earthquakes and volcanoes.

Our economy has likewise developed over time. From simple trades based on a few crafts and a few basic forms of food production we have grown a huge and complex global economy, with its kingdoms of material enterprise and its diversity of species from companies to corporations, living in their balance of competition and co-operation, co-creating and evolving, developing to fill their ecological niches. This is not a story of scarcity and survival. It is one of magnificent abundance, creativity and continual increase in our potential to thrive.

We have brought the system to a perilous state where we are struggling with the complexity of our creation and with its side-effects. It was a feature of the social evolution dynamic that we needed to empower our creativity. But we have failed to do this in a sustainable way because our thinking systems have been rooted in fear and corrupted by greed. We have over-emphasised competition and our way forward lies in rebuilding that system so that it fully recognises the other side of the dynamic and fosters mutual care and co-operation. We need care for our planet, care for ourselves and care for each other. It's perfect that we are where we are, but it's also ripe for change and its time is overdue.

Summary Nuggets

The value of money used to be anchored by its relationship with Gold. It no longer has any anchor at all.

Consumer debt consists of paying for what we desire today with wealth we have not yet created.

The belief in scarcity brings misleading and destructive emphasis on competition alone as healthy and natural.

The truth of natural systems is that they are also systemically collaborative and that they grow in dynamic balance with competitive pressures. This the reality for economies too.

6. Living on the Edge

People don't realise that the Victorian Age was simply an interruption in British History…. It's exciting living on the edge of bankruptcy.

Harold Macmillan

Annual income twenty pounds, annual expenditure nineteen nineteen six, result happiness. Annual income twenty pounds, annual expenditure twenty pounds ought and six, result misery.

Charles Dickens' Mr Micawber in "David Copperfield"

If we are to shape the shift we need to understand the clay we are working with. There are other balances in the economy which we have to recognise and take account of. There is a past-future dynamic between saving and borrowing. There is an extension of the I / We dynamic between the private and public sectors which is strongly present in the stage 5 to 6 transition from strategic drive to human bonding. And there is the ever-present and familiar tension between boom and bust, inflation and stagnation, growth and contraction. All of these are interdependent, and all are ultimately down to us, not to governments.

In the diagram below, the rudimentary spiral portrays the interaction of these three dimensions of dynamics. Human development is in the vertical axis and depicts society's increasing complexity and scale of interactions over time. We have not yet created any machines which are 100% efficient. All of them lose energy somewhere. The bigger the machine, the more energy is required to sustain it. This is true of the economy too. Where it takes 200 people to sustain a tribe it may take 20 million to sustain an industrial economy and 2 billion to sustain a global one. Complexity has an inbuilt cost, particularly if we operate it inefficiently and wastefully.

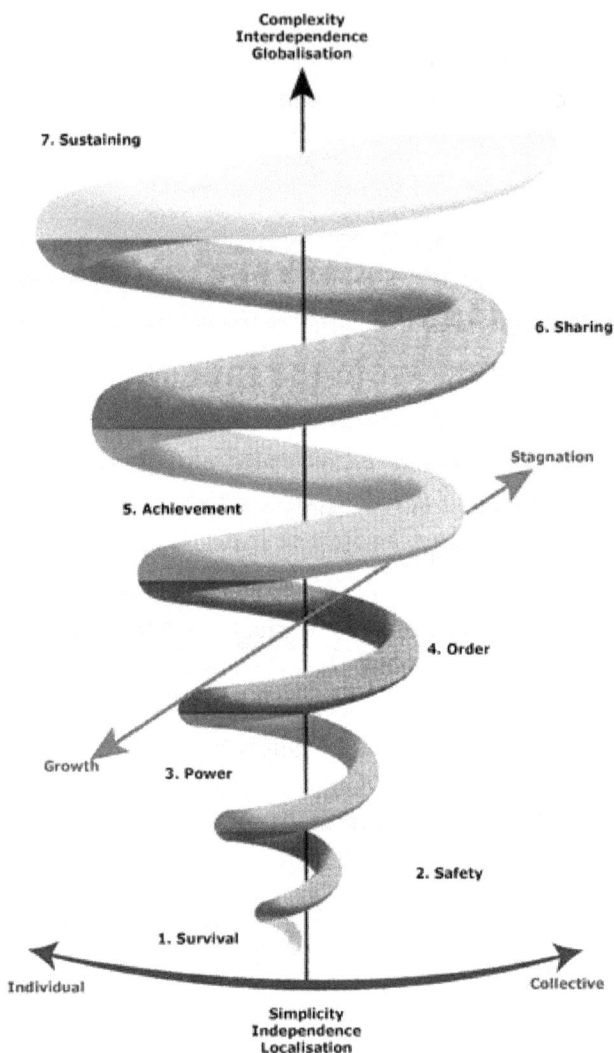

The spiral is in constant flux between the human impulse to express its individuality and the social need for our collective well-being, shown as a side-to-side swing at every level. Not only will this come out in the balance between individual freedom and collective agreement about how the fruits of our labour may be spent. It is present in a continual debate between the public and private sectors in an economy, and this presents a constant challenge, for reasons which we will shortly see.

Equally, at each level there is a tension and oscillation between the impulse to grow and the forces of nature which bring constraint, whether these be represented by the availability of energy, natural resources, or the supply of money itself. Each of these dynamics is very visible in the economic and political conversation and each has to be worked with as we shift to a new level. The supply of money is central to the phenomenon of "inflation" and one of the factors in what form or amount of growth is sustainable.

Inflation and deflation

However much we may be learning that money is not "real" in the way that people think it is, money IS a commodity and is subject to the laws of supply and demand. The economy needs cash to circulate if it is not to grind to a halt. In the introduction where we imagined that all the money disappeared, everything was OK, but this would only be so for a short time. Very soon the world would become paralysed. In this sense, money is as real and as essential as the oil in your car engine – not because it is used, but because motion slows and eventually stops in its absence. But it is also like a catalyst in chemistry – a substance whose presence is essential to the reaction, but which does not actually get changed or used by it. It flows and it lubricates. It is simultaneously essential and insignificant.

We are accustomed to thinking that "inflation" is a bad thing. That is because too much of it certainly is. But in reading coming paragraphs, please suspend the belief that "inflation" should be automatically seen as bad.

If our collective activity is to grow and the size of the engine is increasing then we need more money. But note that it is the flow of the money around the system that needs to increase. If you overfill your car engine with oil, it will actually be slowed down by its weight and its drag on moving parts that are bathed in it. Increasing the quantity of money enables the flow when the demand is there. It does not necessarily produce the demand. If we increase the quantity and there is no demand for flow, then we reduce the value of the money that is there already. It becomes a drag on the system.

As free market economist Ludwig von Mises expressed it in 1951 *"Inflation is an increase in the quantity of money without a corresponding increase in the demand for money, i.e., for cash holdings."* That is to say, when we collectively make more paper money we automatically fuel inflation. However, there is a circular effect. He goes on to say *"I do not mean to say that inflation in itself does not influence the demand for money. The quantity of money and the demand for money are not absolutely independent magnitudes."* In essence, the presence of inflation affects the perception that people have of how much money is needed. Thus, he says *"The demand for money for cash holdings depends on the individual's specific understanding of future conditions—his speculation and his ideas about the future."*

And here we hit the crux of it. While people can argue at length about the mechanics of inflation and how to manage it, ultimately it is driven by behaviour and that in turn is based on our perception. When we attempt to manage the money, but do not manage human behaviour (ourselves) we cannot accomplish fundamental change. The value of savings and the value of pensions, the value of money itself are at the most basic level built on human decisions – shall I spend my money today, or shall I keep it? Can I postpone this purchase? If I can, will the item be more expensive in a month than it is now? Can I put some of my money away for the future?

We hover on this see-saw which is the front-to-back oscillation between growth and stagnation (or contraction). If people think that goods will not get cheaper, they will spend their money. They buy before the price goes up. The money flows and the engine of the economy turns. It is easier to sell goods and prices are able to rise without harming sales. Price rises increase the rate of inflation in an upward spiral. More money is required to keep the engine turning. New species of industry develop. This is growth and potentially increases the richness of life.

In 2011 the recession forced prices down. People could do better by delaying their purchases. The loss of sales forces prices down further, increasing the disincentive to spend. And when people hold on to their money, the engine of the economy does not turn. It is a downward spiral where sales fall, there is no demand for production and people in manufacturing lose their jobs. This is stagnation and life goes out of the system. The death of a company is like the loss of a herd. The death of an industry is like the extinction of a species.

This is the problem that governments have tried to address through Quantitative Easing. But there was a limit to the positive effects which could be achieved by pumping money into the system, especially when people were still in shock and fundamentally pessimistic. Despite the low interest rates which give some mortgage payers a bonus, spending did not pick up. The pump possibly avoided a full-scale collapse and certainly kept the banks afloat. In the end, people's behaviour is a major determining factor. What happens next may well depend on the next balance we look at.

Public and Private expenditures

The public-private balance affects how von Mises' viewpoint may be seen. Because of the growth in state-delivered services, the state has become one of the biggest consumers, making significant decisions about when and where to spend. The significance of individual decisions is reduced. Those who make their money from Stage 5 manufacturing, commerce and trade want the money to remain in that system, because that is where they make their living. They view the government as the enemy of the free market. They want it to do as little as possible. On the other hand, there are now millions of people who make their living in health-care, education, social services and in managing our Stage 6 collective life. Those workers are consumers too. When you hear arguments about levels of public expenditure, you need to know that "government as consumer" is a big player in driving the rest of the economy. The government takes taxes and is therefore the enemy of free-market money flow. But if public expenditure is reduced, only those in the commercial sector benefit. This keeps companies in business, benefiting shareholders (including your pension funds and ISAs). But those in the private sector are also consumers of the services –

they too want their children educated, their bins emptied, their flu treated and their elderly relatives cared for.

In this arena too, we live on a see-saw. We oscillate between governments which believe that the public sector is important and valuable and governments which want to constrain public expenditure in order to maintain the private sector. We are accustomed to this tussle between Republicans and Democrats or socialists against conservatives. The picture gets more muddled by outsourcing (public sector taxes financing private sector companies) and by private sector partnerships. This sits against a deep historical background of "rich vs. poor" and "bosses vs. workers"; many people continue to see the debate in those terms.

In the 2010 UK election the economic argument was between a Labour party which wanted to keep public sector expenditure up for the next year because it believed that taking money out of the economy would precipitate the downward spiral and a Conservative party which believed that deficit reduction is the only way to avoid international perception that the UK is a poor risk, which would drive up interest rates, also collapsing the economy. It is very likely that both were right despite the claims that the UK economy is healthy.

The argument from 2010 persisted into the UK 2015 election. It is at least arguable that a contributory factor in Labour's dismal performance then dated back to its failure soon after the coalition took office, to challenge its assertion that it was Labour's deficits, rather than the banking collapse and bailouts, which along with Conservative dogma brought the need for austerity.

The deficit was thus allowed to be once again the central issue in 2015, none of the parties have an answer and it still remains likely that there will be a breakdown whichever choice is made, whether social or economic. It is undeniable that arguing for austerity aligns with a long-term right-wing desire to reduce the burden on the state. The post-election budget indicates that in the absence of restraining influences from coalition politics that agenda will accelerate. The pressures may yet lead to a political meltdown which reflects these irreconcilable tensions. US voters will also recognise how these show up in different form between Democrats and Republicans as central to political

74

paralysis and federal budget blockages. The 2016 election will inevitably pursue these themes.

Also since von Mises' time, the world has become much more alert and responsive at manipulating the system, managing perceptions through variation in interest rates, taxation and borrowing levels. These mechanisms have been employed effectively for the past decade or more so that the massive hikes in inflation and interest rates which we saw in the early 1990's have not been repeated. The potential loss of economic stimulation that arises from cutbacks to public services will be felt through the whole economy. It will continue to be a tightrope-walk.

Complexity or simplicity

The growth in **complexity** is fundamental to the dynamics of the spiral. But it is worth drawing attention more fully to the nature of this complexity. The increase in scale from tribal to global is self-evident as is the growth of mega-cities and industrial production processes, which apply not only to cars and oil refineries but even to the change in agriculture, where farms too have become huge, mechanised and industrial in approach.

Complexity though, does not come on its own in this scenario. A second feature of modern life is **diversity**. In the west, massive population movement over the last century brings cultural and racial diversity. The effect of this is that the Values systems themselves become more varied. Thus it is not only the prevailing life conditions which drive the way that people think about their survival. People do not change overnight. As the saying goes, you can take the Pakistani out of Karachi, but you can't take Karachi out of the Pakistani. Values systems are embedded. Some aspects will change quickly, but others require generational shifts.

More important even than this is pace – the sheer **speed of change**. This too is obvious and we have a choice as individuals to rush to keep pace, or to create our own insulated niche where we manage our own lives to preserve constancy. But even the most resistant have become familiar with PCs and mobile telephones. But to that we must add the interactions. Comedian Micky

Flanagan, a child of the sixties, talks of a conversation with a teenager who could not understand how people managed their social life without mobiles and texting. "We made arrangements in advance, and we turned up" was his answer. Behind this observation is the reality that we can change our minds and our arrangements at short notice and on a global level. Thanks to 24-hour news I can be aware of significant events anywhere on the earth within the hour. Products come to the market more rapidly and penetrate instantly. The iPod has transformed the music distribution business. The shift from clunky video cassettes to light and postable DVD's meant that movie rental shops went out of business; now streaming is replacing DVD's. Stock market traders are expected to react to events in minutes, and many trades are automated, with computers that act instantly generating hundreds of thousands of transactions every hour.

Under these conditions, **unpredictability** rules. Scenarios cannot be planned, linear top-down management cannot react to conditions on the ground, policies and procedures are outdated before they are printed. The flexibility of today's teenage lifestyle is supported by communications. Protests are organised and mobilised via twitter. Increasingly, commercial organisations will have to build this flexible intelligence and diversified decision-making into their operations.

The implications for this in the money arena are that risk assessment, responsiveness and flexibility are already essential emerging features of the money system. More and more transactions are electronic and systems like Paypal and Worldpay are built in to commercial operations. Paypal has reduced the cost of entry to e-commerce compared with credit card systems. The system of micro-loans with which Mohammed Yunus created Grameen bank and which won him the Nobel Prize is another sign that such adaptation is taking place. Zopa and Dwolla are other interesting explorations, underpinned by the web technology and likely to be followed by many more.

More will yet be required. Money has to flow in new ways and to be connected with many different areas of value for our systems to be adequate. In the midst of this complexity compounded first by diversity and then by speed (or urgency), our physical management of money will need to be accompanied by ways of thinking and decision-making that place increasing demands on us. And in our next chapter we will need to build our knowledge of the way in which money flows. If speed of response is one of the keys, what is required to ensure that flow happens?

Summary Nuggets

There are many dynamics at play in the economy.

We have to balance saving and borrowing, inflation and stagnation, public and private demands and manage the continual movement of our society from simplicity towards greater complexity.

Our ability to manage this trajectory is increasingly challenged by diversity, speed of change, interactivity and unpredictability. Further systems evolution is required.

7. Pace and flow

Trickle-down theory – the less than elegant metaphor that if one feeds the horse enough oats, some will pass through to the road for the sparrows

J. K. Galbraith

One of the hardest aspects of money management and current economics is time. We have already looked at some aspects of our psychology – the way that we get ahead of ourselves and the way that our systems have institutionalized greed. We have also discussed the way that growth and inflation get mixed up. Growth is a real increase in our collective activity. It is not just related to money. When stone-age man sat and chipped himself an axe-head, or tied a sharpened flint to a stick to make a spear he increased his capacity to obtain food, and not just for a day. If I plough the earth in order to grow crops, and tend them and keep them weed-free, not only do I create food, I also add to the capacity for growing future food, by improving the land.

The same applies at an industrial level. The cost of building a truck represents the time and materials that go into it. The value of that truck is hopefully greater than its cost. Even if it also costs money to maintain it, to fuel it and to pay a driver, it is a long-term contributor to the economy – more so the longer it lasts.

A human ecosystem

This is like a living process. When a species colonises a new habitat, it adds to the energy, creating new opportunities for other species to develop. An oak tree can provide a habitat for several hundred species from birds and gall wasps to insects and fungi, not only in its branches, but also in the ground ecology formed by its leaf mulch. Growth is part of life. In the case of an oak tree, the ecosystem may last several hundred years. The taming of horses created an economic system lasting centuries. The truck has not yet demonstrated the same degree of long-term sustainability but it too has spawned economic and social habitats like CB radios, transport cafes and truck-stop diners.

The human population also grows. The planet's growth in capacity to sustain life sustains us too. Through agriculture we create habitats for new food production. Through industry we create new dwelling places. Your home may be 10, 100 or 300 years old and the older it is, the more likely it is to have been built in a relationship with both its own plot of land and with the surrounding geography that would sustain its occupants. Population growth and support-systems growth are directly related. Humans are the same as all other species. If we outgrow support capacity our numbers will drop. Economics is not designed to represent this web of relationships, which is one of the reasons why we struggle to make good decisions when we give money the biggest voice.

Economics is particularly challenged by variation in speed. We represent time in our money systems by counting how much happens over a period. That is, you would value your own personal income by saying I earn $200 per week, or have a salary of $40,000 per year. The country measures its Gross Domestic Product in the same way. For any population we could also represent its needs on such a basis, e.g. this lion "earns" 20 gazelles per year, or this beef cow requires 190 gallons (850l) of water per day.

A beehive "knows" that it has to even out its flow of food. During the summer it consumes nectar, but it also converts some into honey. Evolution has built into its collective behaviour the ability to balance the fluctuating seasons and a successful hive will store at least 40 lbs / 20 Kg to keep it warm through the winter.

Companies may have seasonality too. I used to work for a multi-national toy company which worked all year towards its last quarter, where most of the sales took place. This is harder to manage than, say, a mobile phone operator, who may have a peak in new subscribers from Christmas gifts, but whose call revenues are much more evenly spread. It takes more surplus cash (or borrowing) for the toy company to build up its stock and it runs a higher risk of its sales not meeting forecasts. It can end up with warehouses full of unsold stock in January. More evenly spread sales patterns allow the stock levels to be adjusted, for manufacture to be cut back, and for cash to be flowing through the business on a regular cycle.

Much of the consumer economy relies on Christmas, and a great deal of attention is given to "High Street" sales figures around that time, as a means of taking the economy's temperature. Consumer debt goes up as credit cards are taken to their limits, and any slack is spent in the January sales, when those who got their estimates wrong push through their embarrassing and expensive warehouse surpluses.

Thus annual figures have their limitations. Ideally, families budget their annual holidays and Christmas splurges. Money collects in the system at various times and is released at others. It is not under close control and regulation of the economy has to cope with the ups and downs. But management is not only about how much money there is in the system. It is also a matter of how fast (or slowly) the money is flowing.

Speed and flow

Those who run trading organisations know the simple practicality of this thinking. If you run a business where you have to buy large stocks at high prices, where they have to be stored in a warehouse and invoiced on 30-day payment terms, you need a lot of capital. Your money will be tied up in stock, premises and debt. It is not flowing, and requires a bigger profit-margin in order to be viable. One reason that on-line trading has become so successful is because often those who provide the purchasing site don't hold the stock. Rather they are paying for stock to be despatched direct from manufacturers or centralised depots. They have no premises to maintain and they expect their customers to pay up-front. The operation has low overheads and lower capital requirements and can turn over cash much faster. When the economy becomes more "lean", more can be done with the same amount of money because it circulates faster.

A negative feature of this truth is that it has supported the entire financial services industry. It is easier and cheaper to make money by buying and selling money (which is what bonds, derivatives, pensions and most investments boils down to). Banks traditionally made money by charging to store, lend and pay out other people's cash, in the days before they made more by creating new debt-money. Insurance companies make money by collective management of our individual risks. Other financial organisations have been making money by circulating paper and skimming an amount off the flow. It is the ease with which large amounts could be made doing that which generated the derivatives lunacy. Inbuilt to this lunacy is the danger to some economies including that of the UK, arising from the fact that this industry has become a significant portion of the UK economy, accounting for 8% of output.

Should you ever wonder why governments are protective of it, and reluctant to act on the bonus culture, you only need to know that the finance sector delivers 14% of UK tax revenues. It is also seen as highly "productive" because the added "Gross Value per Head" is twice that of all other economic sectors. This too highlights the core concern, since the "value" being generated is not real in any physical sense. It is productivity without product.

On the positive side, the world has speeded up in many areas, with just-in-time manufacturing, lean processes and the whole e-conomy. The last of these is greatly facilitated by the digitisation of money so that you can now pay bills from your mobile phone, have money go direct from your bank account by chip-and-pin debit card, or pay for goods and services from Paypal accounts and their ilk.

In "*The Zero Marginal Cost Society*" Jeremy Rifkin describes how the emerging Internet of Things is speeding us to an era of nearly free goods and services. His view is that over the coming decades, this will precipitate the rise of a global Collaborative Commons and the eclipse of capitalism. 3D printing is similarly predicted to alter the shape of manufacturing and economics. While these trends are almost certainly influential and transformative and while there may be more such changes to come, they will take time. Nor is it likely that in any future you will be able to print your own washing machine, still less your tablet computer, or whatever comes after it.

The industrial economy will still require scale and will still start in copper mines and sources of rare-earth minerals. Some would advocate that we should give up industrial approaches altogether and return to the land and it is possible that humanity will force itself to do so through collapse. The alternative is that our economy still requires infrastructure and call for large-scale investment in enterprises intended to last for decades. Speed and flow are simple to achieve with electronic transactions and virtual money. What is the difference with industry, and how does "capital" fit into that picture? With this question we begin crossing the boundary between the economics of the large scale and the finance of enterprise. This is where we meet the roots of capitalism itself.

Summary Nuggets

The economy demands that we manage the speed and flow of money in relation to time.

Differing uses and different business models require corresponding differences in the way that money is supplied and used.

Businesses vary in their requirements for investment (capital) and their ability to circulate money.

There is a crucial distinction between making money from goods and services, and making money from moving money itself.

8. The Financial Support and Control of Corporations

"All the problems we face can be dealt with using existing technologies. And almost everything we need to do to move the world economy back onto an environmentally sustainable path has already been done in one or more countries."

Lester R. Brown, Plan B 3.0: Mobilizing to Save Civilization

We have encountered the way in which money developed as a means of exchange and a step forward from the barter system. Money is not capitalism though. So what is capitalism about?

Capitalism expresses something about resource usage. Money which is flowing from person to person is a means of exchanging value. It is when the flow stops that it becomes capital. If we save, our savings become capital, a financial asset. Similarly we can convert our money into another form of asset – a gold bar, for instance. We can also convert our capital into a productive asset. We can buy livestock or a loom or a forge. These have value and the possibility of creating more value and are the earliest beginnings of how capital becomes capitalism.

The core of capitalism as we know it is in how this principle scales up into enterprises, companies and corporations. In rare cases an enterprise may grow organically, generating the additional cash that it can turn into the assets of a larger business. In most cases the extra money must be found from outside, usually through one of two mechanisms. The first is borrowing. The owner takes on debt, money lent to him in the expectation that it will be repaid, usually with interest.

The second is that he finds a financial partner who takes a share in the enterprise. The financial partner takes a personal financial asset and makes it an asset of the business. He takes a risk. In return he receives an agreed share of the value if the business grows. His capital is in the business and in some measure he becomes a part owner. His ownership may be passive – he has no control, no decision-making involvement, because he entrusts the development of the business to the person who created it. Equally his capital might have derived from his own surplus as a successful business person. The partnership might then be active and involve advice, mentorship and influence. It might even mean he has control of the enterprise's future.

Our current system of corporate finance is the above, raised to a much larger scale. In place of a single investor sharing in the company's future there are multiple investors who hold actual shares. In place of the founding owner(s) there may be a whole board of management who make strategic and operational decisions. Founders may still be involved or they may have died, been ousted or happily sold their interest and gone fishing. Or started a charitable foundation.

Inside this simplified presentation sit a mass of considerations which now affect what capitalism has become and how corporations function. Corporations vary hugely in their purpose, their founding intentions, their ethos (or lack thereof), their scale, their ambitions. They may have huge infrastructure with capital tied up in physical assets such as the plant and machinery that Ford require to produce cars or EDF to produce electricity. They may be businesses in which intellectual capital and ingenuity generate fast-paced innovation as with Google and Facebook. Between these two there are big differences in the way that money flows and the speed with which it flows, mirrored by great differences in the amount of capital that is tied up and how long it is required for.

There are also businesses which are critical to the nation. Food production, energy production, water supply and sewage removal might be thought critical to our survival. Transportation infrastructure is highly important to our shared ability to thrive. Different businesses represent differing locations on the axis of public vs private good, and different countries or different times have generated differing choices and blends of public (i.e. government) or private ownership. And of course even private ownership is not simply that when we have collective interests in the investment of our pension funds, life insurance provisions and investment vehicles that we entrust others to manage.

As a result of this there is an extensive list of interests to consider and to balance, a raft of balances to be maintained if the system is to meet the needs of all involved fairly and functionally. And we are all involved, make no mistake.

Here in no particular order is a reasonably representative list of the balances that the system must accommodate:-

- Short-term and long-term benefits
- Investor commitment and investor entitlement
- Ownership rights and obligations to others
- Management control and autonomy
- Regulatory control and flexibility
- Power and responsibility
- Risk and reward
- Private and public good
- Private vs public ownership
- Values and Ethics vs self-interest
- Uniformity and diversity
- Trust vs scrutiny
- Privacy vs transparency

A complete investigation of these would require a full book, not a chapter. Fortunately I do not have to write that book because it has been done persuasively and with great clarity by Prof. Colin Mayer of Oxford University's Saeed Business School in "Firm Commitment". What follows here is a brief paraphrase of his analysis and conclusions. He deserves more and better; I recommend that those who want the full logic should read his book

His central thesis concerns why corporations have failed us and what is required to restore our trust in them. The corporation is one of the world's most important institutions, but also the cause of suffering, poverty environmental damage and financial crisis.

In relation to the balances above he makes it clear that too much weight has been given to incentives, ownership, contracts and control. Not enough has been given to restraints on contractual claims and property rights or to the responsibilities of corporations to third parties – those now typically called "stakeholders". More emphasis is now needed on responsibilities, obligations and commitment.

My own comment on this would be that you could almost think that the system had been devised by and for lawyers. That might simply be a cynical piece of humour were it not that one response to the collapse of trust is the suggestion that what is needed is still more control and regulation. While it is very apparent that regulation has failed we should not assume that more regulation is the answer. Something different might be needed.

As Colin Mayer observes, a survey of 34 directors of Fortune 200 companies reported that 31 of them would cut down a mature forest or release a dangerous unregulated toxin into the environment to increase corporate earnings.[vii] No amount of regulation can keep pace with this problem. Since our future depends on different choices we should look at what drives this reality.

The attention given to shareholder rights is driven by their perceived exposure to risk. They appear to be more vulnerable than other parties to corporate life. Our corporate laws were designed to prevent them handing money over to business owners who would then spend the money as if it were their own. No investment would be made if this lack of security were allowed to apply. They then extend further into an expectation that directors should put shareholder value first in their decision-making priorities – ahead of ethical considerations, for example.

The reality is not so simple. The employees in corporations and their suppliers also make a commitment. In truth, shareholders may come and go while these other stakeholders have an investment in the ongoing relationship. An employee who is let go loses any contribution they made to the company's past success. A supplier who loses a contract may have invested in tooling up or in developing specific expertise. Both may have a lot to lose and if the company ceases to trade neither has a claim on the residual assets beyond any contractual minima.

[vii] From a Study by Jacob Rose (2007) "Corporate Directors and Social Responsibility", Journal of Business Ethics 73, 319-331.

If a company is taken over, the shareholders receive payment. Other stakeholders do not.

The law in the US and UK gives a fiduciary duty to directors – a duty of faithfulness. That faith is towards shareholders. When shareholder value is in the driving seat, executives are duty-bound to maximise this, whatever the risk to other stakeholders. It is also the case that shareholders can remove and replace directors, so they can in effect buy in the executives who will work to the immediate short-term shareholder benefit.

There are numerous results of this distortion. One is that it encourages executives to bend the rules, or even to break them provided they do not get caught. There is evidence that when this happens in the absence of a directly damaging impact on reputation share prices will rise. If the impact is external – on other companies or stakeholders – there is often no sanction at all.

Of course when the victims of corporate activities are third parties like the environment, other species, the atmosphere and water supply there are rarely any direct consequences to the perpetrating corporation. Even reputational damage is rarely lasting, and is often of no influence if the corporation does not sell directly to the public.

The market promotes good conduct, but only in relation to what the market values. There is a direct relationship between Values and value. In a system which has built in the recognition that material values come first, it is inevitable that ethical values or human values come after, if indeed they come anywhere. We have described already how an entire financial services industry has fulfilled that reality.

Another result is that companies themselves are dispensable. Colin Mayer describes how the sale of Cadbury company was driven not by the interests of the company itself, or of its employees, or the wishes of its board. In the short-term it delivered some profit to long-term shareholders – though at the expense of what might have been long-term dividend income. It delivered a great deal more to short-term investors – those who speculated on the takeover – an activity that has no relationship to the company's existence or interests. And if it means that UK jobs are instantly moved by the new owners to Poland (despite assurances that there would be no redundancies) who cares?

Prof. Mayer presents extensive arguments as to why regulation is not the answer to many of the problems we are describing. Often regulations are constructed to fix the last problem, but introduce new ones. Often they distort behaviour in such a way as to produce technical compliance but not improve outcomes. It focuses attention on the regulations and on how to minimise their effects, rather than on the underlying behaviour or the ethos and values that the behaviour derives from. As he says, the conventional wisdom does not hold true. Regulation has unintended consequences that then require further regulation.

I am a trustee of a moderate-sized charity. In that role I am obliged to act in the interest of the beneficiaries, the children and young adults that the charity exists to help. The charity does not have shareholders, of course. It has those who donate, but mostly it is funded by public authorities who pay for the care of those with special needs. Its other main stakeholders are parents and families of the beneficiaries concerned. We have to satisfy both of these constituencies because without them, there would be no beneficiaries and we would be like a company without customers.

I introduce this as a representation of the other extreme of several of the balances above. A Charity is obliged to do many of the things that are absent from shareholder-priority governance. In due course I will discuss how we achieve this – indeed, what is asked of us in order to satisfy regulatory authorities and inspectorates. What if there is a new balance between these extremes?

Understanding risk

We said above that investors take a share in risk with their investment. How true is this? A single investor in a start-up may take a genuine risk. A large investor like Warren Buffett may put a significant portion of his wealth at stake, or the wealth of those he represents. However, Buffett does a great deal of research on the companies he invests in, takes a long-term stake and genuinely knows the business. This is what made him hugely successful.

Even Warren Buffet has spread his risk, however. Not widely and indiscriminately but nevertheless, his investment company may have a stake in 20 corporations at a time. His risk is spread. And within the company he takes a stake in he is not a 100% owner. His holdings may more typically be a few percentage points.

An individual investor in a start-up has a lot of skin in the game. Families have often backed their entrepreneurial members in a big way relative to their core wealth. When stockholders in an enterprise analyse the risk of a new venture that the corporation plans their risk is diluted by however many of them there are, and there may be 100,000 of them. Employees, suppliers and long-standing customers who may rely on that company for something crucial to their own business, may risk everything. Their perceptions are therefore different than those of shareholders who potentially have a license to be irresponsible and to take bigger gambles with the future of their stake. Shareholders are effectively anonymous and protected by diversification.

This again means that giving predominance to shareholders is not supportive to the company as a whole, against the interests of other stakeholders and potentially damaging to our whole economy. A look at the history of companies as a whole – at the rate of aggressive takeovers and bankruptcies and at the frequency of asset-stripping, share-price manipulation and market influence that persuades investors into irrational choices gives plenty of evidence that in its current form the free market breaks companies. There are countries like Germany and Sweden which have a different balance and which don't suffer these outcomes to the same extent. The UK and the US may have something to learn, since the evidence exists that other ways of financing business are indeed possible.

Short and long-term gains

How much energy, time and money is wasted by the frequency of failures, by disruptive takeovers, mergers and reorganisations? I have seen the huge amount of energy that goes into unproductive change. I have also been very aware of the way in which management consultancies drive their revenue by persuading corporations of the need to change their business model.

Stockbrokers and analysts make their living from encouraging churn. Investors who hold their portfolios don't produce the same level of fees. Hedge funds and other investors have a significant interest in creating short-term gains. Stocks reward investors by dividends – a share in annual profits - and by a share in growing the enterprise. Too much power to investor voices can distort the choice of long-term or short-term stewardship.

The current distrust in self-interest of boards is propelling support for calls to increase investor participation and interest. For sure there have been ridiculous levels of self-reward by executives and this will be dealt with later, but the push for shareholder activism is not always driven by such concerns. It can just as easily be driven by a hedge fund that wants to manipulate the company into a change of policy, and which persuades or bullies other shareholders into believing that this represents a rational choice. In most cases such pressures will emphasise the short-term at the expense of stability strategy and long-term growth.

The importance of commitment

The individual who took a stake in his neighbour's business did so for the long term. The shareholder who wants dividend income for their retirement is interested in the long term. They are committed to the future of the organisation.

The stockmarket is not built on commitment. There are computers dictating buy and sell actions that may only last for seconds. At least these do not affect voting too much. But when investment houses are only intending to hold a stock until they have made a one or two percent gain, how much do they justify their right to have a vote on the company's future? There is no commitment. The rights that they have are not in balance with any responsibilities to the company. Their self-interest greatly exceeds any obligations to others and it is unlikely that any ethical values enter the picture. The only value is monetary.

When Adam Smith wrote of the significance of individual choices, seeing the free movement of many participants as constituting, in his famous expression "the invisible hand" he believed that all these free participants, in effect, were society and therefore that their choices even when fundamentally self-interested would nevertheless benefit society.

Unfortunately he was not thinking of today's life conditions and institutional distortions. He assumed a degree of awareness in the individual of the consequences of their actions. He did not anticipate global implications and severe unpredictability. And most of all he did not anticipate the way that corporations would affect the picture. Indeed, he specifically excluded corporations from the principles that he laid down for market efficiency as he perceived dispersed ownership as not conducive to it. Dispersed ownership does nothing to support commitment.

Ending Shareholder dominance

There are more reasons, but the above should suffice to show that we need different ways of ensuring that enterprises of all sizes can fulfil the original potentials that Adam Smith articulated. Smith's vision has been hijacked by people who benefit from license and either believe that it is the same as freedom or who hijack freedom as being only for themselves while limiting or destroying the freedom of others. Most criticism of capitalism comes from those who see its results and believe that freedom has been the cause. As a result they look to constrain or destroy the free market with regulation or social control. That way has already been proven not to work. All the evidence from public ownership of industries in the UK was that they become stagnant, inefficient and ultimately corrupted because the taxpayer picked up the tab for free lunches.

Our most essential industries were nationalised in order to protect the public from exploitation by owners of mines and railways. This rightly addressed in some measure the appalling conditions of mineworkers and contributed to a new balance of power. Subsequently however, in the name of fairness the public purse was plundered for specific powerful groups of workers exploiting the fact that it was that essential need which caused them to be nationalised in the first place.

Our most experience has been that the indispensable industries were seen to be banks. We have all but nationalised some of these through bailouts of those deemed "to big to fail". It may be right that the government should be a safety net but we should be making the necessary changes to reduce the need for one.

There will not be one single answer to the question "how should our businesses be owned and controlled?" Businesses are of many different purposes, sizes, speeds, dependence on employees and resources. It needs to be possible for entrepreneurs to form new businesses from their vision of what is needed and to have flexibility in how they do that.

The attempt to deal with problems in this area through prescriptive regulation will not allow the freedom, flexibility and diversity that a responsive economy needs. The alternative is that we must engage with the values our society desires and embed those. Rather than regulating the specific processes of corporate governance, we should require that they meet our desired outcomes and that they do so from within. That is to say we should expect transparency, probity, accountability, recognition of social benefit, avoidance of harm and fairness to all stakeholders. Shareholder reward and the freedom of the market to find its own levels must sit alongside these expectations.

This is not asking the impossible. It is not even asking the difficult. There are ways in which this already works and good proposals for how to embed it further. We will present these, including Colin Mayer's proposals for In Trust corporations in Section 3.

In leading towards the presentation of what we can do, I would first like to complete our awareness of what has happened to us in the journey through Stages 1 to 6. Much of the above has clarified the way that our fear, greed and desire for control created a system which has ceased to serve us. That internal picture led us towards the mechanics of how those elements are now embedded in our concepts of structure and in how we manage money at the global scale.

We have seen some of the mechanisms which caused the recent collapse and which will continue to make our economic world unstable. We will see more of the detail in our next section as we begin to frame the solution. All of these outcomes are rooted in our stage 4 ordering systems and how they have been broken or bent by the force of stage 5. However we must guard against a backlash. Stage 5 has delivered huge benefits through its explosive force of creativity. We neglect this at our peril. A knee-jerk impulse to smash the system risks taking out the very capabilities that we need to mobilise towards new solutions. As Howard Bloom has put it:-

"But the problem does not lie in the turbines of the Western way of life—it does not lie in industrialism, capitalism, pluralism, free speech, and democracy. The problem lies in the lens through which we see. Capitalism works. It works for reasons that don't appear in the analyses of Marx or in the statistics of economists. It works clumsily, awkwardly, sometimes brilliantly, and sometimes savagely. So we need to dig down to find out why.

We need to reveal the deeper meaning beneath what we've been told is crass materialism. We need to see how profoundly our obsessive making and exchanging of goods and services has upgraded the nature of our species.

The Western system is not at all what we've been taught to believe. This is not a mindless consumer culture destroying the planet in an orgy of greed. It is the most creative and potentially idealistic bio-engine this planet has ever seen. But if we fail to open our eyes and spot this reality fast, everything we believe in may easily disappear."

Our eventual solutions will depend on our willingness to see the above truth and at the same time counter the excesses, to bring the creative and orgiastic together with the idealistic. Our next chapter looks at the heart of Stage 6, at what emerges in the human psyche as it responds to the alienating aspects of our obsessive creative burst. The accusation is that capitalism doesn't care, so how do we re-awaken care and build it in to our future?

Summary Nuggets

The start-up and support of corporations typically requires capital finance.

There is a need to balance the rights of those who provide finance with the rights of other stakeholders.

There is a challenge to manage the relationship between short-term benefits to shareholders and the longer-timeframe benefits of other stakeholders and other forms of investment. This challenge is currently not being met well or consistently.

We are failing to balance financial risk, ownership rights, financial benefits, collective interests and economic value, to ensure commitment to the enterprise itself or to create trust in those who govern them.

Our regulations are designed around processes rather than outcomes, preventing us from recognising or ensuring genuine effectiveness.

9. Re-entering the Garden

In times to come, human beings will have to live for one another

And not the one by means of the other.

By this is achieved the world's ultimate aim

Where each is within himself

And will give to the other what none would demand.

Rudolf Steiner

This book is rooted in a predicted transition and in the evidence that this shift is underway. There is much that has been portrayed as broken and no longer fit for purpose. Several of the facts and predictions could provoke some fearful responses. But I do not intend this to be a pessimistic book. While the transition demands massive changes this should be seen as an optimistic message, not a gloomy prediction.

As stated, the need for such a major transition arises from complexity, an effect of growth in scale, diversity, communication, interactivity and speed. Without doubt those factors have made the change urgent. But those same factors make us the best informed, most aware, most connected global human population that has ever existed. We have the tools, the technology and as Lester Brown states, we have the knowledge. All the solutions already exist and are available to us. The challenge is to put them together and we need to engage the will to do so.

The historical picture is one in which we have allowed money to become master. We have made it into a god, and developed belief systems in which we put the money first, signed up to a collective belief system that if the money worked, we could all be happy. Since this has not worked, the transition also demands that we change our belief systems. Einstein famously said that you cannot solve a problem using the same thinking that created it. The injunction on all of us is to think differently.

> *This planet has - or rather had - a problem, which was this: most of the people living on it were unhappy for pretty much of the time. Many solutions were suggested for this problem, but most of these were largely concerned with the movements of small green pieces of paper, which is odd because on the whole it wasn't the small green pieces of paper that were unhappy.*
>
> *Douglas Adams, Hitchhikers Guide to the Galaxy*

The God of Money has died. The crunch signalled his demise. His body, to be sure, is taking a while to decay but he is not coming back even if there are many who refuse to give up the belief in him. The money-first world is coming to an end because it has neither made us happy nor established a means by which billions of humans can live sustainably. On the contrary, it threatens to destroy us. Fortunately the answers to both sustainability and to happiness have the same source.

The Judaeo-Christian religions are remarkable, possibly unique among human cultures for having produced a mythology in which humanity has been expelled from the Garden of Eden. In the book which tells this story, God had previously blessed humankind, instructing male and female to be fruitful, multiply, and replenish the Earth. He has also in the King James Version instructed us to subdue it and to have dominion over every living thing. Perhaps a more modern translation would grant us stewardship or guardianship. We have to take care of it.

Cultures which have remained closer to the natural world continue to recognise themselves as caretakers of the garden. It would seem that when we gave our power to the God of Money, we left the garden. It is time for us to return. Our way back is by replacing a money-first world with a care-first world. All the items on our list of requirements for a reinvented capitalism will be fulfilled when both our thinking and our systems embody that care, when we apply the principle of stewardship to balance the needs of all life. Those requirements arise out of a choice to care for each other, for ourselves, for the planet's other life-forms, for its resources, for its climate and its oceans.

The Bible was no doubt both written by and translated by men. Expressions like "subdue" and "have dominion over" come from the masculine side of our nature. If it had been written by women and from the expression of the feminine side of our nature, we would have recognised that the earth already provides abundance. The sun shines every day and everywhere that humans live there are resources to live by. The inspiration behind the following images comes from my friend and collaborator Louis Böhtlingk. As he would say, the Goddess of Abundance is with us. We have set up and served an illusory God of Money; for the Goddess to thrive, we must now replace him with a Prince of Peace. These two, our feminine and masculine expressions, can now work in harmony to produce a Care First world, to re-enter the garden and to take up our stewardship of it.

During our journey we have examined the illusions that humanity has taken on. We have given too much attention to our fear, losing trust in the natural world and in one another. We have allowed our creative urge to tip over into greed. We have adopted a scientific viewpoint which however brilliant it is at exploring mechanics and components, is filled with misunderstanding about life as a whole and which has encouraged beliefs in scarcity and destructive competition. We have failed to see the rich collaborative interactions which generate species diversity and ecological balance; as a result we have failed to apply this perception to our economic balance. Organic life itself has generated all the species of the earth from what was originally a mineral soup. As Ken Wilber put it, "dirt got up and wrote poetry". Our economic growth could reflect that living creativity if we could put our care ahead of our fear, our greed, our selfishness, our possessiveness and our tendency to confuse "power to" with "power over".

The tree of life

Some of the images used in this book have been mechanical, relating our economy to engines and bicycles. Re-entering the garden, another image might be more appropriate. Cars can be built, but trees have to grow. Their growth is responsive to their material conditions and it is governed by an inbuilt intelligence. This is a more useful indication of what our economy requires.

The "workers" in a tree are the leaves. They take the energy of sunlight, the carbon dioxide in the atmosphere and the water from the soil, and convert it into stored chemical energy in the form of sugar (glucose). They take the Hydrogen from the water molecule and liberate the Oxygen. The sugars are used by the cells of the tree to provide the energy that they need. The "energy pack" inside each cell (mitochondria) breaks down the glucose, recombines it with Oxygen and liberates the stored energy – but now as chemical energy, not sunlight. Both water and carbon dioxide are released back into the system. These activities are the foundation for the web of life, powering the Earth's food chains.

The tree also takes other nutrients from the soil, using the energy it is generating to build new cells. Over time, these new cells become the infrastructure of the tree - its roots, trunk branches and leaves.

Science does not know where the intelligence of a tree is to be found but the tree as a whole is responsive to its environment[viii]. Its root systems spread according to the structure of the soil and the nutrient sources in it; in addition they connect

---

[viii] The reasons why science is half-blind are dealt with at great depth in my previous book "The Science of Possibility". ISBN 978-0956-01073-5 (paperback) plus Kindle and ebook.

communicatively with other trees. Its branches grow in such a way as to capture the most sunlight. Lower branches are shed when the higher canopy blocks the sun. The trunk develops strength according to the winds it is subjected to; trees grown indoors do not develop their strength unless manually shaken. When water is scarce, the tree will shed leaves in order to limit water loss. And the tree will also bend the shape of its growth to orient towards prevailing light. Trees succeed in sustaining their form and growing it, in some cases for centuries. Science may not yet understand their intelligence but we must.

For our economic life we require a similar capability to manage our relationship with resources and for our growth to be sustained and sustainable. In the image above, water is the money supply for the tree. It transports nutrients and is used in transactions, but is always recycled, whether internally or through the atmosphere. Gradually the tree increases in size because it builds its structure, sequestering carbon and other chemicals. Anyone who has nurtured a tree also observes that initially it does little above the ground. Its energy goes into its roots, both to secure it against the wind and to stabilise its nutrient and water supply. An economy needs its money supply to be secure and its resources to be available. Growth follows after root development. A tree which does otherwise does not survive the next gale.

How fast can a tree grow? One thing should be obvious; you cannot make it grow faster by watering it excessively. Lack of rainfall will hold it back but the real constraints are in the supply of energy and raw materials. In the economy there is human energy – people willing to work. There is energy supplied by consuming natural resources like oil and coal (our "ancient sunlight" as Thomas Hartmann calls it, stored as sequestered carbon). There is energy from today's sunlight and the motion of the heavens (wind, tidal and wave power). And in addition we have harnessed the power of creation in nuclear form with its attendant problems of toxic risk and waste disposal.

We know that we don't have a problem with the amount of our natural resources. We know that we do have a problem with which ones we are using, and with oil in particular. Even so, our human resources are huge. We have the capacity to get things done and we have enormous creativity in finding ways to do them better. As a result, we have grown a lot. The planet sustains more and more humans (leaves) every year. The root system has grown in support with more mines, oil rigs and agricultural productivity. The trunk has increased, with our stock of buildings, plant and machinery, cities, sewerage and drainage. We have a very large and varied transportation system.

At the same time we know that we face a crisis. The tree is not growing straight. Its branches are one-sided, massively larger on the North and West than on the South and East. This species of tree requires oil and has put down very deep tap-roots into a resource that is struggling and must eventually fail. These roots will die. It needs to send out shallow roots into alternative energy sources, but is not growing these fast enough. Its soil is becoming waterlogged, over-watered with too much money that weakens its hold in the ground, while the leaves are filled with water presenting maximum resistance to the wind. How long will it be before a severe gale, perhaps one from the South-East, blows it over?

The intelligence of the tree is challenged by this scenario – pushed to the extent of its capacity to change. How fast could it grow branches on its weaker side? What resources would have to be diverted to achieve this? How much water (money) must dry up – remembering meanwhile that if water gets scarce, the tree will have to shed leaves?

We are reaching the limits of this image, but have pushed it to emphasise the requirement to find an organic and non-linear response. In nature a tree has the intelligence to respond to its environment. It shapes with its surroundings, bending toward a one-sided light-source, sensing the presence of water and minerals and growing its roots toward the best sources. It may have broad flat leaves which it sheds during the winter to protect it from frost, conserving itself when light is low. It may have narrow, tough resinous needle-like leaves which protect it from frost. These responses took billions of years to evolve and they may take decades to operate.

The tree has the intelligence to do this but does it so slowly that we cannot see its thinking. Roots and branches grow cell by cell. Humanity has to respond more quickly and we have the capacities. Our rise as a species has been so rapid because of our flexibility and adaptation. We are the tool-making, thinking animal; we are the animal with the biggest brain and the opposable thumbs, the animal which can adapt the environment to ourselves. That is our strength so inevitably it also contains our weakness. Our environment has its own intelligence, its own balances. It may "think" more slowly than we do but we are seeing what happens when we behave as if we are more intelligent than it is. We are finding out that we were not quite as smart as we thought, and nature is certainly not as stupid. We need to listen to it.

We have been greedy, but we have also been prideful. There are still people who believe that we can solve all of our problems with technology. While we will undoubtedly solve some and mitigate others, we are still in Titanic mode, racing at full steam towards New York. The lookout is shouting "iceberg". The owner is pretending the ship is unsinkable. What does it take to slow the liner and turn it around?

The answers are already there. Many of them are contained in "Plan B". Lester Brown's visioning offers a practical roadmap through investment in energy efficiency and carbon reduction, through population stabilization, the eradication of poverty and by restoring natural resources. Here we have pointed to proposals that shift the dynamics of the economy – shift them away from greed, away from the preservation of historical self-interest, away from rewarding toxic behaviours. These suggestions shift the economy towards balanced engagement with all the planetary stakeholders, fairness to all its human and non-human inhabitants, stewardship of its resources and sensitivity to its climate. The tree responds to the seasons. We need the capacity and intelligence to respond to global warming or to the next ice age regardless of whether we are creating them or merely affected by them. We need to know what is beyond our control.

There is a well-known prayer which runs "God grant me the serenity to accept the things I cannot change, the courage to change the things I can and the wisdom to know the difference". For our current situation we need a little more than this. Acceptance is the starting point for adaptive response. We may not be able to change the world, but we can change our response to it. We can manage the consequences. We can change ourselves.

Our modern age has been light on Faith. In a stage 5 materialist world, God is an endangered species. This may in part be what allowed us to put the false God of Money into the gap. In one sense losing the old stage 3 and 4 Gods may serve us. If we think that God is "out there" we may become passively accepting of our fate, pondering what sacrifice might change His mind or falsely trusting that He or someone else will sort it out. If you are a believer there is at the very least a need to accept that we have been given free will and that it is not too late to use it – to ask "what does God need us to do?" Stage 6 is humanist; we start to look for the God in ourselves and in one another. It is something to hope for that this will support us in making the transition to a Care First world.

Our return to the garden, or perhaps our recognition that we never really left it, is a shift in consciousness. That is to say, Conscious Capitalism starts with us. We will see that Stage 7 takes us beyond both materialism and humanism and calls us to care for both ourselves and the garden. (It is typical of stage 7 and beyond to demand an end to either-or thinking and its replacement by both-and responses.) The mythology of the Fall describes humanity as becoming separate from nature and from the Divine as a result of our engagement with knowledge. There are many ways to interpret the biblical words but my view is that we have placed intellectual knowing above intuitive, instinctive knowing, above the promptings of our hearts and our inner awareness of our connection with all life.

When presenting Care as a conscious choice, I do not mean to imply that this takes us further into the intellect or perpetuates the excessively masculine dynamics of recent centuries. Care is natural to us when we are not inhibited from it by fear or driven by greed and lust. The conscious choice is our first step, our deliberate decision to put the money-first world behind us. What follows has to be a re-engagement with the feminine, the heart-centred knowing that engages our deep humanity. That instinctive response is also the one which feeds the human spirit, reawakens our love for ourselves, for each other and for the Earth.

Human beings have evolved with a special form of intelligence. It is an addition to the inbuilt organismic intelligence that evolved over the eons, not a replacement for it. Only in a narrow sense is it a "higher" intelligence. Like a child with a new toy, humans have been over-excited by it and have played with it at the expense of others. Like the sorcerer's apprentice we have grasped a form of power which we have half-mastered and which is teaching us hard lessons.

What will it take to shift our consciousness and raise our capacity to the next level? We will need our intellect and even more our capacity for awareness. Our stewardship may be heart-filled but it is not mindless. We will need all of our capacities, including some that we have forgotten. We will need our technology too. While we need to harmonise once again with nature we will continue to need the many tools that we have developed but to apply them with greater wisdom and understanding. We will need our science, but we must extend it beyond its current capacity so that it understands that some aspects of the material world are not visible, that the laws of the Universe are paradoxical and that humans are meshed with a creative dynamic that is itself intelligent. And we will need money. We will need a fair, flexible and responsive system with which to express our real Values and support our sharing of the Earth's Gifts.

At the close of his Vision for a Care First world, Louis Böhtlingk describes the four actions that we can make in order to bring about the transition from one level of experience and consciousness to another.

First Action: To move from a place where we try to get and take our piece of the Gift, towards standing around the Gift together and receiving and sharing in it.

Second Action: To move from ownership to stewardship.

Third Action: To move from a use of money based on our greed, fear, power, selfishness and possessiveness to a use of money based on caring, sharing loving, giving and receiving.

Fourth Action: To move from a Money First attitude to a Care First attitude.

The purpose of this book so far has been to show just how the Money First world developed, how this reflected a natural development in human Value systems, and to show how the mechanics of our economic life reflect those Values. We now need to show what Values will be required to solve the problems we are experiencing and to indicate some elements of the new mechanics that will be required. It has been stressed that the shift comes from within and the actions that Louis lists are foundational aspects of that internal impulse. Out of that impulse we can individually and collectively take the steps which will deliver a sustainable form of economic life and a healthy version of money.

We have allowed a series of illusions to develop: the illusion that money represents the real world; the illusion that the problem is with other people; the illusion that the world functions on competition; the illusion that the control is outside of ourselves; the illusion that the answers will come from our leaders.

Since none of these things are true, it follows that there must be other truths: the truth that money is merely a tool to enable our human relationships and is not the reality; the truth that we are the problem and the solution; the truth that the world is by nature creative and collaborative; the truth that we have power and control over our destiny and that it is up to us to provide the answers. In what follows this book offers a basis for making the choice, an outline manifesto for what is needed and some pointers towards answers that are already waiting for us to use.

Summary Nuggets

Emotionally the transition that we face is one from systems built on fear, greed, desire for power, selfishness and control to systems based on care, collaboration and co-operation.

Our model for the use of money has been mechanistic and has failed to represent the planet and the economy as living systems.

Our way of using money has prevented us from seeing the true value and relationships to the resources we are using.

A Care-First World would get us out of the habit of thinking that everything will work right if we manage the money.

Section 3: Systems that support new Values

We should be thinking not just what is good for putting money in people's pockets but what is good for putting joy in people's hearts.

When politicians are looking at issues they should be saying to themselves 'how are we going to try and make sure that we don't just make people better off but we make people happier, we make communities more stable, we make society more cohesive.

David Cameron, BBC Radio 4, May 22nd 2006

That sounds really good David.   How's it going?

Great British Public, July 2015

10. Money: Lubricating the Capitalist Engine

If economists could manage to get themselves thought of as humble, competent people, on a level with dentists, that would be splendid.

John Maynard Keynes

As we discussed in chapter 8, capital can be viewed as real or financial assets that possess a money value. Real capital is a physical stock of productive assets – buildings, machinery, infrastructure, arable land, livestock and software. Financial (money) capital represents all the non-material assets, including cash, securities and debts. A company may also be regarded as having assets such as goodwill, intellectual property and brand value but we will not treat those as capital here. At the simplest level, real assets are those items that remained during our exercise at the start of this book when you were invited to imagine a world where money had vanished. Since we represent both forms with the one kind of money this recognition alone is a challenge to our financial thinking.

A look at company figures presented in annual accounts shows that there is an attempt to distinguish these different types of money, sometimes referred to as revenue and capital, and to separate them. A Profit and Loss or cash-flow account shows the flow of money through the organization as it traded through the year. Its balance sheet shows what it owned at the year end, a mix of what has been invested in plant and machinery, and what it might also be valued as owning if it were sold as a going concern. This would include items like goodwill but also negative items like debts or provisions made against costs of making good after a catastrophe like the BP Gulf Horizon oil-spill.

Accounting rules are extremely complex and have developed over the decades in an attempt to make visible all the aspects of business which affect a company's value. But they are a long way short of the ability to reveal risks (like those of the BP oil-spill), the ongoing environmental impact of the company's operation, or its long-term effects on planetary resources, societal function or human health and well-being. Consider then, how effective we can be at evaluating the state of a whole economy.

Even the above picture of a company or an economy struggles to indicate the pace at which money is moving. The level of a company's debt is visible as a proportion of the company's value, and at the national level this is also known. There are coarse measures that indicate pace because the ratio between turnover and the cash employed to produce that turnover does broadly indicate how fast money is circulating. But for large organisations and for entire countries, there are many variables to consider and the fluctuations are rapid. Even using computers, relationships are hard to track and even harder to predict. Fundamentally the complexity is beyond the capacity of almost all of us and that probably includes most of those who think they can cope with it and whose job it is to do so. But even if we grant them full understanding we should look at the tools they can use to manage that flow and at who has the use of those tools.

Regulating the flow of money

In the US, the Federal Reserve sets the interest rate for the whole economy. In the UK this is done by the Bank of England Monetary Policy Committee (MPC) and most countries have central banks that do this. These institutions are tasked with regulating the flow of money. They have just two levers to pull. One controls the amount of money in circulation and is the lever that was pulled in 2009 under the name "Quantitative Easing". Some people would call it "printing money". The other lever manages interest rates. These bodies attempt to regulate money flow in order to prevent inflation and are required to anticipate what will happen, taking action to cool the economy when inflation threatens. Cooling is done by raising interest rates to discourage borrowing so that we do not get too far ahead of ourselves.

At a national level, our economic well-being and the rate of inflation are affected by many factors. Here's a few of the big ones:-

- Oil prices, which affect the cost of manufacturing and transport of goods, as well as domestic budgets. Note that other commodity prices have similar effects

- Exchange rates, which affect the direct cost of imported goods (raw materials, food, consumer items)

- The level of wage demands (potentially a circular affect, since demands will be related to expected inflation levels as well as historical ones)

- Sales taxes and other duties

- Interest rates themselves (also a circular effect)

- The international climate of opinion regarding our value; will global investors buy shares in UK Plc or yourcountry.corp? Will they lend money to you (buy your government Bonds) at viable interest rates?

When you note that oil prices and exchange rates are very volatile and outside of national control, it is clear from the outset that prediction is very difficult. When the whole system is pressurized, fragile, prone to speculation and may at any time be affected by severe shock (anything from the next volcano to a bank collapse, disease outbreak, political event or terrorist incident) those two levers look like very blunt instruments. Try texting while wearing oven mitts. Similarly, when confidence collapses, as when Italy needs to re-finance in order to service the 2.3 Trillion Euros that it owes against an ongoing deficit and no growth prospects, nations can be very vulnerable. As we saw earlier, Italy is a microcosm of the total world economy, owing more than it can possibly repay.

Of course national institutions like the Fed and the UK MPC are not the only players in the global economy. Big companies are buying and selling currencies in order to trade. They too are anticipating their oil and commodity needs and making long-term buying decisions. Large financial institutions are moving huge amounts of money from company to company and country to country. Your pension may be invested in China or Brazil. To some extent these many attempts to predict and anticipate can have smoothing effects, where one action is rapidly counterbalanced on account of its expected consequences. At the same time, the complexities are beyond any tracking mechanisms and the interactions between the known variables are not susceptible to good analysis. You only have to listen to economic bulletins or read blog conversations between members of the investing community to discover that none are operating on better than "best guess" basis.

Where does money come from?

It is conventional to believe that new money comes into circulation via

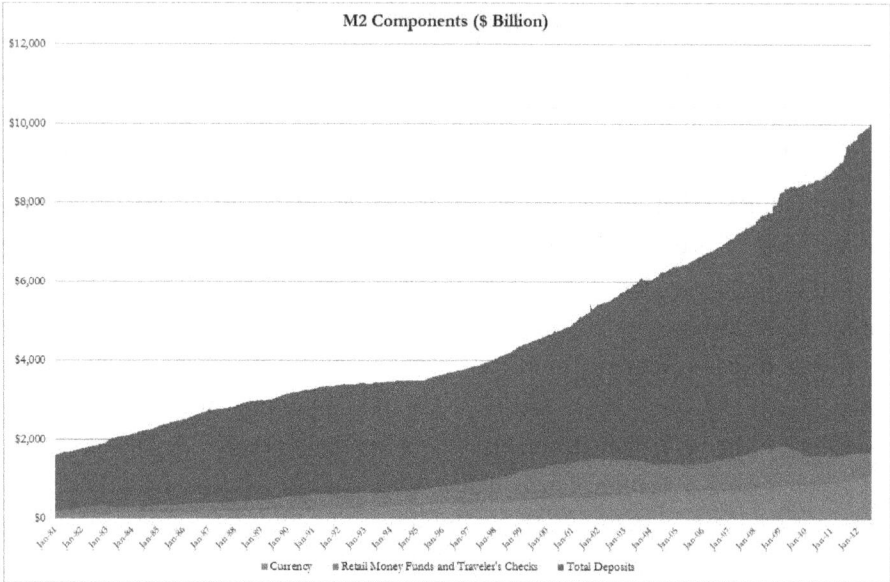

M2 Components ($ Billion)

governments. Only they can "print" new currency. This is still true, but while currency printing used to be the only source of new money it isn't any longer. The banks are also issuing money because banks are able to issue debt. Banks can offer you money that has not yet been printed and may never be printed. They can offer you money that you are expected to earn in the future, money that may yet be created by economic growth.

In the graph depicting the US money supply over recent decades, the two lowest bands represent the money in US currency and current accounts. The third band labelled M2, is the money issued by private institutions. Forty years ago, the currency and current accounts were half of the money supply. Today they are about 15%. This means that over three quarters of the new money has been issued by banks and other institutions. In reality the picture is if anything worse than this since M3 which is no longer calculated includes the really big loans such as the credit given by banks and home loan providers as well as money held overseas by US residents.

The UK operates in a similar way. In the UK, banks only have to possess approximately one-twelfth of the money they lend. That is, 92% of their lending is unsecured. This has given them the latitude to pump money into the economy. In 2008 the amount they added to the money supply was £200 billion. 97% of all money in the UK is digital money, not currency issued by the Bank of England. Large proportions of this money went in housing loans. Largely through this mechanism these amounts had been increasing by about 7% per year through the previous decade. Since creating new money is a primary cause of inflation, it is hardly surprising that this created a housing bubble.

The law of supply and demand applied, and since new house builds are generally below 1% per year, more and more money chased proportionally fewer houses. Prices rose accordingly. (Note that in effect the banks themselves were fuelling the guaranteed annual rises on which derivatives were "secured".) This is a worm which feeds on its own tail. Equally significant here is that much of general consumer borrowing is then fuelled by our perception of the personal wealth we see in our houses.

Also in the UK, it is estimated that of the new "debt money" pumped into the economy by banks, only 8% (yes, less than one tenth) is loaned to productive business. So the new money doesn't even fuel the real UK economy. The remaining 92%, besides going into the housing bubble, fuelled other paper speculation and encouraged consumer spending. While some of the latter feeds into the productive economy of goods and services much goes overseas, often to Asian manufacturers.

The sad truth is that it is easier for banks to lend to consumers. They don't have to apply the staff time and expertise to understand your business plan. To maintain the illusion that it is less risky than a commercial loan it suffices to check that you have a job and that your automated credit report is satisfactory. And if you ask for a small temporary overdraft it is easy for them to bring up this information and persuade you that you can afford a bank loan for a new car or kitchen. Those sales are heavily incentivised. Staff members don't get high bonuses for cautious lending! The sales of loans generate commissions, they show as turnover and the money you owe appears as an asset of the bank.

Such offers of extra money are hard to refuse so consumers find themselves encouraged to take on the maximum possible debt. Part of the imagined security also relates to home ownership – the bank assumes that your stability is underpinned by your house value. But when that is artificially inflated, when the economy slows, when people are on short-time or laid off and when the value of housing starts to drop that security vanishes into the ether. Both the banks and those of us who were seduced by their promises, become very vulnerable. In some cases that vulnerability is concealed. I know personally of two people who told their lenders they were no longer able to pay. They were told that the bank would not pursue them, but would keep the debt on the books rather than close it. Who knows how much money still shows as book assets when in truth it is a write-off?

Laws that make it illegal for you to print your own £5 or £10 notes have been in place since 1844 in England. But those laws haven't been updated to account for the fact that almost all money now is electronic. Because of this loophole, banks worldwide now have the power to create money, effectively out of nothing. In the US, Congressman Denis Kucinich proposed changing the law to take this power back from banks. In the UK, a campaign ran unsuccessfully with the intention of closing that door here. It is no surprise that bankers can pay themselves £5 billion in bonuses each year. That is a mere 2.5% commission on the money they are (not) printing (or debt that they are issuing).

Nor is it a surprise as we saw above that this sector of the economy prides itself on being the most productive. I too can be very financially productive if you allow me to create my own money. And I would even be happy to pay tax on it so that the government has an incentive to grant me that privilege. Be assured though, that the result of the inflation this creates is that our housing costs much more than it should and that the debts we are incurring as a nation are growing since we are steadily devaluing our currency. It is one of the fundamental reasons why you cannot be sure that any money that you have made and which may be sitting in digital form in an accounting system somewhere is worth the paper that it is no longer written on.

The first money had a value that was socially determined in relation to real goods and services. Now it is impossible to know where the value lies. It isn't determined socially, it's not set on our behalf by governments. Most of it probably has no value at all, which is why financial collapse is unavoidable. It isn't REAL money. It isn't FUTURE money that can be paid back at close to today's value. It's UNREAL money, all but worthless. I call it FUNNY MUNNY, but it is deeply sad.

Taken all together, this is why we are struggling. Don't take it from me though; take it from Mervyn King, recent Governor of the Bank of England who says *"of all the many ways of organising the banking system, the worst is the one we have today"*. We have a complex set of variables which we are attempting to manage at country level using inadequate tools. We hover not simply between growth and depression but on the edge of stability, undermined by a system which has made money-supply growth into an institution whose main beneficiaries are those who issue the money and unaccountable to the rest of us. It is like a formula 1 car, approaching a bend too fast and hovering over the brakes, at the edge of losing traction and spinning off the track. And the driver is drunk.

We have a global economy which runs on fear and competition, where those who manage it walk a tightrope between the individual (country or multi-national) self-interest and the collective interdependence. We have a system for managing the money supply which is clumsy even under good conditions, but which is undermined from within by the very banks on whom we supposedly rely for care of our money. Or what used to be our money. We cannot turn this system off overnight, but we can start applying the brakes, and we can begin to apply the remedies which are available to us.

Summary Nuggets

Governments (and the Central banks that nominally serve them) no longer have control of money creation.

Banks are creating money through setting up debts inside their systems which are not backed by real currency. They have replaced capitalism with debtism.

The money created by banks has fuelled debt and housing bubbles to the detriment of society as a whole.

11. Capitalism, fairness and the flow of money

"To forget how to dig the earth and to tend the soil is to forget ourselves."

Mohandas K. Gandhi

Throughout this book we have been viewing evidence of the ways in which money is broken and needs to change. At the same time we are not able to do without it. The existence of money does not automatically imply a capitalist system so we need a further look at the nature of capitalism itself and at the core of how we operate money.

Capitalism has come to be thought of in relation to Communism – as its opposite and as the political system that the USA and Western Europe have adopted. There are value-judgements involved in this choice, ones which have led to wars and to decades of deep hostility. There are still Marxists around for whom capitalism is a pejorative term which describes a system in which one class of people own the means of production and a second class of people does not, having merely the capacity to work. Communism is merely one example of an approach to money which does not imply capitalism.

Communism is not the answer

This is not a Marxist book. The world has changed a lot since Marx's time, and with our pension funds and investments we are all capitalists now, though this does not change a fundamental and obvious truth that there are some individuals with more power over the money than others. Nevertheless attempts to implement Marxism have shown very effectively that shifting the money and the ownership do not by themselves prevent the abuse of power. This is because the Values systems are more influential. Stage 3 power relationships and Stage 4 state bureaucracies characterised the Soviet era and concentrated huge power in the hands of the Politburo and the KGB. Demonstrably that system prevented the emergence of a healthy Stage 5 and post-communist Russia is still stuck, now in oligarchic power. Chinese communism is navigating that transition now with a mix of success and unsolved problems.

Reinventing Western Capitalism calls for the consciousness to build it on Stage 7 Values of systemic, flexible, complex thinking. When the downsides of capitalism come under attack, the best defence offered is that it has proved itself to be the "least worst" alternative. This lazy and ostrich-like posture is inadequate to our situation, fails to recognise just how bad things have become and is often driven by the same short-term self-interests as are under attack. But it is not helpful to demonise the finance community as "spivs" and "criminals" for their personal Values systems when these are our Values too. We will all have to change in order to develop the new systems.

Where Marxists would once have identified an in-country capitalist class and a local proletariat, today we are dealing with countries and multi-nationals which own the means of production and other countries which predominantly supply the labour. In the 1920's workers fought for wages and fairness. Now each country manages its local and short-term interests, so when our leaders gather for Kyoto or Copenhagen, the inbuilt tensions are unmanageable. The labour-supplying countries are fighting for their "wages". That is, they want to catch up with the rich in terms of housing, electricity, education, health and personal aspirations. An ambitious Nigerian girl may now want to study to become a doctor, not because she wants to help her country but because she has seen the Western lifestyle on TV and wants her share. We have no right to criticise her for this because we have all been party to selling her that dream.

Global communism is not the answer. But it is appropriate for us to recognise that the tensions which have existed for the last two centuries have not gone away; they have merely relocated to a higher level. From slavery to sweat-shops, from alms-houses to Live-Aid we continue to deal with the same in-built issues, embedded as they are in our thinking and our Value systems. As well as changing that thinking we may need to look at the lessons we learned during the last century at the national level and evaluate how they apply internationally. For example, one response in the UK was to nationalise the (then) major energy supply – coal - and transportation system – the railways. Neither of these was ultimately successful, even if miners did for a while become better-paid and more powerful. Global energy ownership in such a form is not a likely solution, but the likely eventual dispute over Arctic Circle oil and gas reserves is not something to welcome either. Our current approach to ownership embodies Stage 3 power struggles, sometimes with a Stage 5 commercial overlay. It is not enough.

We must start from where we are

Thus the bottom line here is that while money itself is essential, the capitalist system as we know it has passed its use-by date. We need to address a belief and a system built on the existence of inequality and constructed to preserve the status of those who have previously obtained special and privileged positions. The sources of that privilege may vary from fighting battles in the 14th century to, sleeping with royalty in the seventeenth through slavery, exploitation of the third world and industrial dominance in the 18th, 19th and 20th. Today's UK Prime Minister David Cameron is descended from an Earl six generations up his family tree and both he and his possible successor, the Mayor of London Boris Johnson, are believed to be illegitimate descendants of King George II (b. 1683). Other countries may not have monarchies, but they have their equivalents, their Kennedy, Rockefeller and Bush dynasties. This is not to condemn either, merely to recognise that in Spiral Dynamics terms we may be entering Stage 7 with Stage 6's sensitivity to inequality while the echoes of Stage 3 power structures and Stage 4 social orders travel with us.

There is nothing fundamentally wrong with having made money and wishing to keep it for the benefit of one's family. Nor is it wrong to reward brilliance, creativity, hard work and commercial risk-taking. There are also deep traditions and values which are embedded in many countries where the aristocracy may be custodians of history, land and buildings. This analysis emphatically does not lead to proposals for a revolution where the wealthy are murdered and their property stolen. That is not a moral solution and it can't even be justified as a means to an end. As Russia showed in 1917 and over several subsequent decades, it doesn't work.

Imbalance between countries

Many countries have introduced a progressive principle which is embedded in the principle of inheritance taxes, in higher taxes for higher income bands and in the expectation that those with most have a responsibility towards those with least. The major religious systems espouse moral principles around fairness and responsibility to one another and even in a world where God is an endangered species, the morality still applies. Unfortunately the problem is now not simply a matter of class systems within countries but of deep divisions between countries. The same applies to corporations and nations which built their wealth and power by exploiting the Earth's resources, often in other lands than their own and while enslaving the populations that lived there. South Africa was built on these gold-plated and diamond-studded foundations and the apartheid regime was for many years the means of holding on to what had been seized. We live on the legacy of empires.

It must be clearly understood that the response to these historical realities must not be intended as some form of revenge or retribution. People in the past did what they did, for good reasons and bad. Now we must acknowledge that this is not how we need to live in the future and that a system which structurally perpetuates those inequalities on a global scale has reached its end-of-life. Balance needs to emerge quickly, ideally without catastrophic conflict. For that to happen many people will have to give up something. Some must give up power and dominance. Some must give up their resentment and desire for revenge. All of us will have to deal with our fear, greed, selfishness, guilt and desire for power.

Imbalance with the planet

If further reason was needed, these imbalances are now playing out across the globe in an imbalance between the human species and the other tenants of planet Earth. The money system as it is now has developed to perpetuate plunder, lack of care for each other or the ecosystem and the maintenance of privilege. We must distinguish between systems which support those who are creative and industrious to achieve and generate benefit from those achievements, and systems which merely support those who plunder historical inequities to live off the proceeds. When such systems also inhibit our ability to deal with pressing problems such as terrorism, global warming and unsustainable ecology we can no longer ignore their other weaknesses.

118

In chapter 3 we encountered the historical prohibition of usury by major faiths. This ban has been undermined or overturned for the benefit of those who wish to make money from money – to have money grow simply because it is there. An investment in a venture is a risk, a creative act where you make money from success, from supporting entrepreneurialism. It uses capital to propel real growth. A loan does not involve the same degree of risk and interest rates typically far exceed the risk of default. They may be secured in the way that mortgages are but even when not secured the return is built in to the agreement. Religions, viewing abundance as a gift from God would accordingly expect that giving to be extended to others.

The principle of usury, where those who have money exploit those who do not, extends beyond the mere possession of capital and the lending of it. The lending of money for interest was a primitive and early form of usury. Now usury is embedded in the legal and economic structures. Those who began the industrial world have taken the right to extend that dominance across the globe and the international laws on ownership are designed to protect that position. We need to take seriously the resemblance of this position for multinationals to that of the 19th century mill-owners. Their position was not sustainable and neither is ours.

The word "oligarchy" denotes "a form of government in which power effectively rests with a small segment of society distinguished by royalty, wealth, family ties, military control, or religious hegemony". America lives in the illusion that it is a republic and a democracy and even names its political parties in accordance with this belief. It recently elected a black president against all odds, but the scenarios playing out since then show how quickly the historical power-base re-asserts itself. American politics have never been about who is President and always about who owns the President. This is a potential recipe for deep conflict, as voters see their democratic hopes stamped on and as the vested interests reassert dominance through ownership of media, financial muscle to buy advertising and influence, and the huge political lobbying industry. The technical term is "plutocracy". The Obama phenomenon caught them out and they are looking for revenge, ensuring that he is paralysed until they can re-establish control. Both before and during his time, the money has continued to flow from Middle America into the pockets of the top 1%, as has been outstandingly well documented by Arianna Huffington in "Third World America".

Just as the political empires were forced to retreat by independence movements through the second half of the 20th century, economic empires are under pressure now. The "BRIC" economies (Brazil, Russia, India, China) are already exerting that pressure. Russia has huge strength despite its years of industrial failure because of its small population relative to a huge landmass and natural resource base. It rivals the middle-east in oil production and has one of the two major supplies of the potash on which industrial agriculture depends. The others are already visible in their growth, and while they may yet face some of the growing pains that the West went through before them, to some degree they stand on our shoulders, and start with computers, mobile communications transport systems and many other industrial lessons that took the West decades. Brazil in particular is also learning from our experience and is building-in sustainability.

An investment adds to the flow because it stimulates productive activity. Loans and credit are more likely to stimulate only consumption. Even house purchase has become a consumer activity, as is indicated by a swathe of property makeover and house-hunting TV programs. The trend has to be reversed. Money which is not gainfully employed needs to be redirected and the concentration of historical capital needs gradually to be redistributed.

Capitalism and the new currency

I have used the image of money as a lubricant for the engine and the water in the tree. At the same time, capital is the money which pays for new investment or which finances the ongoing operation of the business. It becomes more than a lubricant because it creates a new engine. It is sequestered in the next tree that grows. Capital has two sources; either it is a real surplus from the past (that of an investor or from re-invested profits) or it virtual, borrowing from our future, virtual money made available on the assumption of growth to come.

If we are to balance ourselves between the past and the future it will not be enough that we reduce or place limits on our tendency to lean forward too much and run too fast by borrowing from the future. We also have to ensure that we can unlock the past. The economy of the future will need to be more responsive to change than we can currently claim to be. An excess of vested interests will threaten our capability to deliver the pace and flow that is needed. We will only get the required responsiveness into the system if we loosen up.

Interest is something that rewards people for holding on to money. What would happen if we rewarded people for keeping the money moving?

When deciding whether to make an investment, a key concept is employed which calculates the expected value of that investment in today's money. In order to turn the complexity of various costs and benefits over varying timescales into something easy to see, formulae are used which work out what the value of that money would be right now. The result is called a "Net Present Value" (NPV). If the NPV is negative, the investment would lose money. If positive, it makes money. Depending on how big the positive value is, one investment or set of assumptions can be compared with another to determine which is of greatest benefit.

The receipt of interest on money sitting in a bank gives a disincentive to invest – particularly in the short term. It counteracts NPV. Inflation is affected by the uncontrolled and unpredictable expansions to the money supply created by bank credit. This makes investment decisions more uncertain because NPV is less predictable. It is harder to know what the future money will be worth.

There is an alternative to this way of operating, sometimes called "demurrage". Jordan Bruce MacLeod, author of "New Currency", a fine book on the subject, calls it a circulation charge. There is also an article in Kosmos Journal that summarises his views, available online[ix]. It is an idea originally proposed by Silvio Gesell as a mechanism which would increase the velocity of circulation and offer a counter-weight to inflation, hoarding and interest. What it also does

---

[ix] http://www.newcurrency.org/blog/circulation-charge/hello-world/#more-1

121

is influence human thinking with a subtle shift from what we get by receiving money towards what we gain by giving it.

We might think that buyers and sellers are in an equal position but Gesell's view was that the owner or the supplier of services is not in an equal position to the purchaser who has money. The person who has cash can sit on that cash until conditions are favourable for her to make a purchase. Time is on her side. Similarly the person with goods may be subject to perishability, storage charges or obsolescence. The person with services to sell loses out every day that those services are not used. Time is not on her side and urgently so if she is unable to buy food or pay her rent.

Gesell proposed a new currency to be issued by a body separate from the banks themselves. The only function for this new institution would be to issue money when the economy needed it and to remove money when it had too much. This new currency would be issued in much the same way that central banks print money now to stimulate the economy. Over a period of time, it would replace the old currency, which could be exchanged for it at any time. But instead of paying interest on borrowed money, the recipient would be incentivised to spend it. The new currency would depreciate by one-thousandth of its value every day (approximately 5% per annum). In order to keep it valid at its original worth, the owner of the currency would be required to buy stamps from the bank and add them to the note.

The miracle of Wörgl

In 1932, the mayor of Wörgl, Austria, was suffering from a 35% unemployment rate in his small town. With a long list of projects and only 40,000 Austrian schillings in the bank he used this small cash reserve to back the creation of local currency with a unique feature. In accordance with Gesell's design its holder would pay a small fee each month to keep it valid for circulation. Once the fee was paid, a stamp was placed on the back of the paper note to certify it for exchange.

The mayor of Wörgl then used this currency to begin paying for public projects, thereby introducing it into the town's circulation. The effects were not immediate, but after this money was spent they began to accumulate. In less than two years from the start of the circulation charge, Wörgl became the first town in Austria to reach full employment.

As described by money expert Bernard Lietaer, the man credited with the invention of the European currency system, these were the results. "Water distribution was extended, the town was repaved, most houses were repaired and repainted, taxes were being paid early, and forests around the city were replanted." Clearly, when a town begins to experience full employment during a depression and citizens voluntarily decide to pay their taxes early, something unusual is taking place. The town's revitalization garnered international attention and was branded the 'miracle of Wörgl.'

While the town gained some revenues in collecting fees from the circulation charge, this was not the source of the transformation. Rather, it was the change in behaviour of Wörgl's citizens. Because of the monthly expiration date the average velocity of money throughout the town increased fourteen-fold as compared with the national currency. This was the source of their remarkable economic transformation- until their national government shut it down.

This kind of dramatic leap in economic activity and confidence cannot be replicated by central governments through spending programs or tax cuts. While it can be looked on as a miracle, the achievement was backed by solid innovation and grounded economic strategy. When we consider our recent financial gridlock this type of charge offers a powerful economic tool to stimulate lending and thereby melt frozen credit markets.

In one sense, demurrage's effect is similar to that of a negative interest rate on all currency in circulation; like inflation, it reduces the purchasing power of money held. But a circulation charge does so through fixed, regular fees while inflation does so through expansion of the money supply. Money supply expansion is less certain in the magnitude of its effect, involves an unpredictable time for it to develop, and is not necessarily uniformly fair in its net impact upon the holders of the currency. In contrast, demurrage operates on a known, regular schedule, in fixed amounts. These certainties make calculation of NPV more certain, and encourage long-term investment.

It would now be easier than ever before to implement a circulation charge, and certainly a far better approach than quantitative easing. The system by which stamps had to be added to the Wörgl currency would nowadays seem too clumsy for viability. It would be relatively easy though, to implement such a system digitally. If it operated alongside an existing paper currency which was steadily being withdrawn, and where the trend towards cashless "chip and pin" and touchcard types of transaction continues, it would be possible to phase the new currency in over a 5-10 year period, bringing about a step by step shift in the balance of the economy. A beneficial side-effect of this change would be to make money-laundering and crimes which depend on cash more difficult to conceal.

In his book "The Future of Money" Bernard Lietaer gave examples of different currencies that have been used in the past or are being used, and the positive and negative effects they carry. He champions the view that in order to optimally solve problems and create a healthy society, the world needs a wide variety of currencies in its "toolbox", and that otherwise we are "painting with a screwdriver". He proposes that the new currency should be global, calling it the "terra". Potentially this has an additional benefit in acting as a stabiliser against currency speculation, and introducing an anchor which fulfils the role taken for a long period by the US Dollar after the gold standard was abolished. It also revisits John Maynard Keynes proposals to the Bretton Woods conference, but in a multi-currency world, does not stop the existence of local economies. We will return later to the question of the Gold standard, and of the balance between a "reality tether" and a system which has elasticity, flexibility, accessibility and velocity.

Motivation is crucial. The Austrian government shut down Wörgl's experiment because it did not serve their purposes. Perhaps more specifically, it put power into the hands of the citizens because there was a currency that the government did not control. Potentially attempts to recreate the Wörgl experiment would also offend governments. For one thing, they won't like economies that they cannot tax. For the citizen, the circulation charge causes a major shift in motivation because it causes us to think differently about money. The balance between negative motivators (fear, greed and control) and positive motivators (creativity, sharing, caring and giving) is altered. What might we be able to do – even if it challenges our governments – to increase the number of alternative currencies with in-built impulse to circulate?

Among the reasons why nationalised industries failed is that without the stimulus of competition the impulse to be efficient and deliver high quality was reduced. In moving to a world in which the impulse to care rises above fear and greed we need to replace negative motivators with positive ones. This is a highly complex exercise in human psychology in which simplified views of human nature are unhelpful and naïve; typically they lead to one-size-fits-all solutions. They are not aligned with the facts of human development as revealed in the Spiral Dynamics developmental sequence. Many individuals will continue to live from the Values systems at levels 3-6 and will be motivated by the rewards that match those values. Motivators have to be relevant to them or they will not motivate!

For example the stage 3 warrior Values system seeks immediate gratifications. Deferred rewards are of no use to them. Stage 4 is the one in which "rewards in heaven" are meaningful; they are willing to defer gratification and find praise satisfying, where Stage 5 achievers are more likely to seek the tangible evidence of status and material reward. While our long-term goal in a care-first world is that all should be doing the right thing because they are internally motivated, because they want to serve customers well or take care of the planet, this is not a realistic short-term prospect. External motivators, whether regulatory sticks or bonus carrots will continue to be required. Competition and care can be present together; in fact such a combination of factors more accurately resembles the evolutionary ecology described during our re-framing of Darwinism.

Most of all, a tax on money which is "held on to" would have a gradual effect in directing the use of capital into productive avenues, or encouraging its release into other parts of the economy. Charitable giving would also be likely to increase. But it needs to be understood that changing the system is only a partial solution and that many other changes would be required. Demurrage is just one example of measures that can be taken, and all measures will need to rest in an urgent shift of thinking and attitudes.

Summary Nuggets

Our currencies have been a one-size-fits-all mechanism that is insufficient for a complex economy.

The way that we think of money and the systems with which we represent its value encourage hoarding and inhibit flow.

We are unable to manage the relationship between the rights associated with past wealth and the creation of a fair future with a level playing-field.

At this time, those who have money are able to behave in ways which stifle competition and creativity and prevent fairness to emerging nations.

A mechanism which ensures that hoarding is penalised, and pushes money into productive use would benefit the entire economy.

12. The end of the linear

Human beings, who are almost unique in having the ability to learn from the experience of others, are also remarkable for their apparent disinclination to do so.

Douglas Adams

"There are only two truly infinite things: the universe and stupidity. And I am unsure about the universe."

Albert Einstein

Stages one through six in our spiral portray a trend of structural development. The first four have clear lines of command. The leader of a band (1), the elders in a tribe (2), the warlord or gang chief (3) and the king, bishop or president (4) all have firm control. Without him (and it has most often been a male) a decision was simply not a decision.

In the more strategy-oriented stage 5, this remains true, but the hierarchy beneath the leaders begins to be less linear. Army chains of command and old corporate silos where any division was only represented through its top general or director begin to break down. Some decisions cut across the vertical structure. Marketing and manufacturing people can talk to each other – within limits. Information Technology is across everything. But only in Stage 6 does hierarchy really begin to dissolve. Stage 6 is more concerned with human bond than with status, so hierarchy starts to give way to community and consensus. This can create major tensions between it and the lower stage Value systems. It is also inadequate in practice for any decision-making which is urgent, involves significant numbers of people, or issues which are complex. When the building is on fire, you do not want a consensual discussion on which exit route to take.

More perhaps than any other, Stage 6 can be looked upon as one which is transitional. It is the dawning of our awareness as individual, self-guiding humans (the teenage-like individualisation that began in Stage 5) that we are each required to take a piece of the collective responsibility. For the first time our societal choices are not determined by parent-like forces (chieftains or bishops) but by ourselves. We are emerging into adulthood and our own accountability, both to ourselves and each other.

As a result the current stage of our societal evolution takes us beyond the realm where all decisions can be passed up and down the chain of command. This linearity is too slow and too inefficient. Often the amount of information that can be passed (or that people choose to pass) will dilute the quality of the decision-making.

The traditional methods of communication are also breaking down. In the linear structures chieftains spoke to their tribes and popes could issue encyclical decrees. In the last century communication was still top-down and centre-out. Even while newspapers gave way to cinema newsreel, radio broadcast and television, only the medium changed. The same people spoke and the same others listened. To some extent they still do; the Murdoch empire persists.

More recently digital media and the internet are changing this beyond all recognition. Social networking creates interaction in all directions, and information is generated by anyone with a mobile phone / video camera / netbook. Opinions are blogged and passed virally throughout interest groups, collectives and societies. There is a new generation which does not read newspapers.

What can the internet do?

We do not know yet what this level of connectivity may do for us as a species. There are some who regard the internet as the nervous system of our collective intelligence. This is not true yet, not beyond the level of a prawn. Note for instance that alongside the apparently consistent use of English there exists an internet in Chinese serving a quarter of the world's population. In the global organism, cells are perhaps forming into clumps. They may even be developing the rudiments of organs and later we will discuss the exciting emergence of loosely structured collaboration but there is no overall functional coherence yet. Towns, cities and states do not function as organic wholes. Some companies do a little better, but even they struggle with internal tensions and difficulties in ensuring that all parts are in service of the whole.

A healthy human body would not have the problems that the human species has. It would not be arguing about whether to send oxygen to the left foot or the right. It would not decide to put all of its energy into digestion and give up breathing. When it puts its hand on a burning ember, it removes it without requiring any time for a decision. When we think of our intelligence we are aware of our capacity for conscious thought. We tend to forget the much greater level of intelligence that is built in to all mammals – the systems which all the time are managing our oxygen flow, our water balance, our temperature, the systems which replace millions of cells every second, the systems which overcome bacterial invasion or which turn food into fuel for cells, the systems which make cats so agile and enable humans to play the piano. These are a small sample of the things that the body does every day.

Some of these systems operate through the brain. Some are regulated rhythmically and energetically by the heart, which sends more information to the brain than it receives. Every organ is sending chemical signals to other organs through our neuro-endocrine system. Hormones are flowing through the body, influencing activity in every cell. When you decide to get up and walk, your body will respond as a whole organism – sending fuel to the right muscles. Your lungs will breathe faster than when at rest. It would be helpful to have another word than intelligence with which to make the inbuilt knowing that lies in the billions of cellular decisions more distinct from our conscious thinking. But intelligence is what it is. The body knows what to do.

This is the kind of image that we have to hold if we are to move from simple responses to linear problems into the multi-factor demands of the complex world. If you fall and scrape your knee, the body knows within seconds what it must do to inhibit blood loss, what chemicals it must send to support blood clotting and scab formation. If we view the internet as global nervous system we may be getting to the point where we know immediately that damage has occurred somewhere on the globe, but that is the easiest step. We are not yet at the point of immediately recognising what resources are needed to address the problem. Still less do we have the delivery mechanisms instantly able to mobilise and deliver those resources. But worst of all, we currently behave as if there is a decision to be made. The body's response is autonomic and instinctive. When your child falls over, or is about to run into the road, your response is immediate. The response of love and care is not debated. It is automatic.

Likewise if you trip and scrape both knees the body does not indulge in a lengthy argument between the two about which is more important. The internet does not yet have the level of connectivity that allows us to know and respond organically to global needs. Even in relation to our current crises, there are dozens of groups and agencies formed around individual agendas, all competing for space, lobbying for the interests of wildlife, or carbon management or new forms of energy and within that, debates about solar power, wind turbines, tidal schemes, wave harnessing techniques. Many have important pieces of the puzzle, but we are only in the infancy of our ability to join the pieces. And at the moment there are some pieces of the puzzle in active resistance to any joined-up picture. The oil lobby has not wanted to play, and no-one can be sure where a nuclear industry fits or if it should even be in the picture. And all the while the picture is changing. Tomorrow, a new technology may shift the balance of our energy choices. How quickly could we assimilate the new knowledge and re-orient our decision-making, much of which is long-term with significant lead-times and investment choices?

It will take intelligence at all levels to create a world in which all the needs are satisfied in a way that brings us back from the edge. This book has spoken a few times of Global Bankruptcy. Bankruptcy is the state that exists when your debts massively exceed your assets and ability to pay back. Since you have to look hard to find anywhere that is in fiscal surplus, this is not in question. Everywhere has a share of the derivatives debt, or the bond market or a pensions deficit. The world is mortgaged to the hilt, and facing a drop in income. Some time soon, we will own up.

The good news is that in bankruptcy it is only the money that can be lost, at least to start with. We will be in the scenario that you imagined at the start of this book. However in our images, money was the oil in our engine and the water in

our tree. The bad news is that without oil, the engine cannot run and seizes up.
Without water the tree sheds it leaves. Our first challenge is to be in a position
to restart the engine before serious damage is done. But that is only the
beginning.

The need to deal with multiple levels simultaneously

The edge we must pull back from has been repeatedly stated. It is the
combination of environmental, ecological, social and political pressures in a
fast-changing interdependent world. Economic collapse will bring a knife-edge
like that of the great depression. On one side there is the challenge to keep things
going – to get food and fuel into cities, to get waste out of them, to prevent social
breakdown, to continue healthcare, support for the old and weak and provide
education. We will all be dependent on one another if we are to prevent total
misery.

On the other side is the world crisis. The last great depression created the
conditions for WWII and witnessed the same social tensions and anti-Semitism
in Britain and the US as it selectively remembers in Germany. Our response this
time will need to be different, and even if we keep things going, we must
transform the world, redefining ourselves and building systems that take us
down new and sustainable pathways. Regardless of suggestions that we should
change the big picture in matters like currency systems, it is of no use to wait
for the big changes. The real transformation must come at every level. The big
changes are helpful enablers which can improve our ability to find flexibility
and balance, but without our own personal change, bringing them about depends
on the same people who led us into this swamp. More significantly, the world
economy is driven by us, by billions of us making daily buying and lifestyle
decisions, making long-term plans for ourselves and families. It is driven by
thousands of small, medium and large businesses making choices about what
technologies to invest in, how much attention to give to the environment and
how to respond to the multiple needs and pressures that they face.

As stated this requires a deal of consciousness-raising. For organisations there
are simultaneous shifts in structure, functional process and leadership style
which correspond to images of organic life and its inbuilt intelligence, of tree-

roots "deciding" where to grow and human organs operating coherently. This intelligence did not evolve in nature as a top-down process and it cannot do so for our species as a whole. In nature it came about via small numbers of cells together in slime molds and primitive organisms, developing over time to the complexity of the 50 trillion cells that make up your body or mine. This is a bottom-up process. Human intelligence on a planetary scale will arise from competent cells grouping together, developing their own local intelligence and the communication systems that facilitate response and flexibility.

New management approaches will be required. Spiral Dynamics integral, in addition to predicting the requirement to manage complexity has also developed the approaches which enable us to do so. There are several toolkits which provide the understanding that map and integrate developmental stage complexity, align and distribute processes and teach the leadership skills that are required. Under names such as "Meshworks Solutions", Barrett Corporate Transformation Tools and Integral Leadership Framework, these approaches are also backed by assessment and information management systems that build the knowledge base and connectivity which this kind of intelligence requires. Frederic Laloux tells the stories of several inspiring examples in his recent book "Reinventing Organizations (2013). Typically these are Values-based approaches which recognise complexity and avoid polarised thinking. We will deal with the support of business organisations more fully in the next chapter.

At the same time, other developments are taking place which will serve to counteract the excessive centralisation and global thinking which rob us of the sensitivity and responsiveness to local conditions. Transition towns seek to create sustainable local economies. Michael Strong and John Mackey's strap line speaks of "how entrepreneurs and conscious capitalists can save the world". Jon Miller and Lucy Parker are similar; their strap line to "Everybody's Business" is "The unlikely story of how big business can fix the world", though their examples show that it is only unlikely because we are not yet doing enough of it, not because there is an inherent problem. Their book is filled with details of how some of the biggest and perhaps least expected companies have been creating first-class examples of what is possible. Grameen bank has already empowered millions of individuals to transform their personal economy. The bumper sticker which exhorts us to "Think Globally, Act Locally" is very much to the point. We will all need to find out what is happening locally and to become more engaged, even if only in small ways. The proposal for subsidiarity and distributed democracy is relevant here. There are corresponding needs to "Think Collectively, Act Individually". In Stage 7 and 2nd tier systems we must each connect with the wave and act as a particle.

The massive structures which have been created during Stage 5, whether these are cities, states, social infrastructures or multi-nationals, have brought big benefits. But they have also created concentrations of power and decision-making which are too unresponsive for the conditions we are describing, and sometimes corrupted by self-interest. These concentrations have also led us into ways of thinking that do not serve us and they are not yet conducive to non-linear responses. Many people have come to see themselves as controlled by these big forces, helpless in the face of their influence, victims of what they are doing to us and to the world. These mindsets need to end. We are not victims; it is not someone else's problem and not somebody else's fault. We cannot afford to allow ourselves to be small and none of us is completely without power. It's down to us and however imperceptible our individual influence may appear, collectively we make a difference.

The Law of unintended consequences

Edward Tenner's book "Why things bite back" takes a deep look at our inability to predict the effects of our actions. If you have heard of antibiotic-resistant strains of disease or spend parts of your day in traffic jams caused by our rapid transportation systems, you know that there is a law of unintended consequences. I reviewed this paragraph on a day which reported a 62-mile traffic jam outside Beijing, destined to last for several days – possibly weeks.

We are not good at predicting what will happen, particularly where the future is concerned. We fail to recognise the limitations to our knowledge and we have a history of discovering that things were not as simple as we thought. The world is more complex than our thinking systems can manage. To a large degree we need to replace thinking with awareness. This is a different skill and those who

133

wish to know more may like to look at the work of Steve and Chutisa Bowman[x] as well as at "The Science of Possibility" which gives the reasons why it is more effective. Some steps in this direction have already begun in the adoption of "Mindfulness" and "Presencing"[xi] approaches.

Discovering our predictive failures also has perverse consequences. Each new technical breakthrough continues to be hyped and oversold. At the same time, we are now chronically fearful that we may be caught out. We now experience the cost of mitigating risks, of testing everything to the hilt, of applying Health and Safety rules to a point of absurdity. We are now terrified of getting it all wrong. One answer is that we require sensing and monitoring systems which are quick to reveal when choices must be adjusted.

We are also slower than we need to be in adopting new technologies. This may seem a strange statement in a world of i-phones. But the pigeon-hole method of organising papers invented in 1789 didn't become common until 1820[xii]. While we use our technology for social networking, our bureaucracy – even its name says "office" – relies on paper-oriented systems, even when digitally stored. Such systems are too cumbersome and too expensive, but hard to eliminate. As Howard Bloom says *"It took over fifty years before Henry Ford found a way to elevate the American System of interchangeable parts into the assembly line. Who will pull off the new Ford-like synthesis of Internet and personal productivity tools? Who will do for the smart phone, the laptop, the iPad, Google, Skype and Wikipedia what Ford did for the tools of manufacturing?"*

When paralysed with fear we cannot deal well with a complex and fast-moving world. In Paul Hawken's stunning May 2009 commencement address at the University of Portland he said *"Forget that this task of planet-saving is not*

---

[x] http://nomorebusinessasusual.com/about-the-book/

[xi] From the work of Otto Scharmer and "Theory U".

[xii] http://www.kurzweilai.net/is-the-ipad-the-new-guillotine : Howard Bloom

possible in the time required. Don't be put off by people who know what is not possible. Do what needs to be done, and check to see if it was impossible only after you are done."xiii

There will be many reasons given for not doing the things suggested in this book. Those which are reasoned may be countered or, where real, mitigated and overcome. Those which are merely based on uncertainty of outcome are more dangerous as they delay us from doing what we can at a time when uncertainty is becoming our most reliable state. Since scientific knowing is limited, and our ability to predict is often illusory, we must learn to accept that life involves risks and to put our energy into responsiveness. We will have to learn to move fast enough to react to the consequences as they become visible. We will also need to become better at using our intuition to sense those things that we know, but can't say how we know them. Flexibility, adaptability, communication and distributed intelligence are essential. We will have to become more conscious.

It is certain that by the time this book reaches printing and distribution the conditions will have changed, and highly probable that we will be experiencing the financial breakdown and possibly others. It is in the nature of the systemic complexity that it is impossible to know precisely what the trigger will be or when it will activate. It is even more difficult to anticipate where and how the consequences will be felt, what attempts will be made and by whom to rectify the emerging problems. Whenever this inevitable crux occurs, we will see graphically for ourselves just what it is like to move out of linearity, to experience perfect storms and chaotic outcomes.

It will be all too easy to see these circumstances as disastrous, which they may indeed be for some individuals. But we need to endeavour to see the opportunity and to recognise the turbulence as the creative force of a new world. If and when you find yourself facing these conditions, remember to be part of the solution, to be resourceful, to band together and to care for yourselves and each other. Money will not provide the answer because it does not connect our intelligence

---

xiii http://www.up.edu/commencement/default.aspx?cid=9456

135

to one another, and does not raise our level of consciousness. Care and awareness do. They are the key at every level, and will be the subject of our final chapter, after a discussion of the way in which the manifesto and non-linear thinking come together in the future life of business entities.

Summary Nuggets

After Stage 6 in human development we need a new way of thinking in order to manage complexity and interaction.

Linear cause-and-effect models are inadequate to deliver responses to fundamentally chaotic systems.

Our decision-making must adopt shorter horizons, be more willing and able to adjust, offer sensitivity to multiple variables and balance analysis with intuitive awareness.

We need to behave as interdependent parts of planetary living systems and not just external controllers of them.

13. The Corporate perspective

The only way managers can win is by making their employees win, because they are the true value creators.

Vineet Nayar   CEO of HCL Technologies

Most of our attention thus far has been either towards the large scale of national and international thinking or toward the contribution made by our individual attitudes. We have not focused much on commercial organisations. Many of the dynamics we have discussed in relation to financial institutions show up in companies of all sizes and many of the effects of our wonky thinking are delivered into the world by them on a day to day basis. Organisational change holds many of the keys to transformation and the shift hinges a great deal on what they do.

Free-lunch fantasies and the belief that growth must be continuous and never-ending have been powerful economic drivers. Leaders have found themselves imprisoned by market expectations and under pressure to take whatever steps will satisfy the demand that every quarter should out-perform the previous one when, as Kip Tindell of The Container Store observes "It's conscious capitalism, not quarterly capitalism". It is rare to hear an executive express the ambition to find the optimum size for their company, and to be healthy, vibrant and maintaining competitiveness by continually improving quality at that chosen size. It would be even rarer to find shareholders and board who would support such an intention, which probably can only occur under private ownership.

This requirement for perpetual growth becomes a hamster-wheel. When executive egos are engaged and personal achievement is measured by it the drive is intense. Market leadership may also become a primary measure of achievement. The recession has presented an opportunity to rethink. It presented to many a challenge to shrink gracefully but there is no sign that the market will accept this for the future. If anything the demand is for more

137

expansion in order to recover the lost ground. The systemic lessons about what gets us into trouble remain unlearned.

The effect of these pressures is to force company leaders into irrational behaviour. In the era of easy borrowing it was all too tempting to use debt in order to expand and to buy market share. Jack Welch, CEO of General Electric is known to have said that being number 1 in your marketplace is essential. Aside from the perverse consequence that this led his executives into regular redefinition of their marketplaces, narrowing them to where the demand was technically still met even as performance reduced, the danger of this philosophy should be obvious. More significantly since there can only be one winner, this cannot be a good strategy for the majority and neglects the nature of ecological systems. The effect of such thinking often persuaded companies to cut prices in order to buy market share, driving down profits. This is not an imaginative, creative or quality-oriented approach and if an entire industry competes on that dimension even the last one left standing may be severely damaged by the journey. The market-share imperative caused companies to borrow in order to fund expansion that was unsustainable, leaving them exposed to failure or buy-out. Such a drive for market domination is also damaging to minority needs as niches disappear and one-size-fits-all thinking increases. It is good that the "best" should find its way to market recognition and that poor quality, poor service and poor fit to needs should meet with failure. At the same time "best" is not always best for everyone. Healthy life exists in diverse ecologies.

Welch, whose success was built on much wider managerial strength that supported his "number 1" ambitions, eventually changed GE's approach to focus on growth. But growth too works only if profitability is also maintained. Growth, particularly if financed by borrowing, does not necessarily create value, profit or wealth. The danger of putting growth above everything is that you periodically over-build. When times get tough this can be catastrophic. There is a perverse effect here too. You can add to your current gross product by manufacturing large quantities of stock, but if these cannot be sold (whether through over-supply from competitors or market shrinkage) then you are destroying value and reducing profitability. Building office blocks adds to GDP, but it does nothing for the nation's wealth when large numbers stand vacant.

Thus market share and growth both have their downsides and must be balanced against a recognition that sustainability and profitability have to be present too. Ultimately our effort and endeavour must make something that is of value to others. Growth in particular is part of a short-term focus. It is not realistic to imagine, still less to demand that any enterprise can always grow. Basic common sense tells us that it is against nature, which is cyclical and subject to ebbs and flows. And if we lack common sense we need only look at the history and at a century of stock market charts for proof.

Another negative effect of concentration on market share and growth is the compulsion to increase the size of organisations. This sounds at first like a good thing to do. The idea of economies of scale is a familiar one and holds an important core truth but like most truths it too has its counterbalance. The tendency to overbuild can apply to the organisation itself. It may become bloated, sluggish and too big to respond to change. This has always been a challenge but in today's world our familiar themes of complexity, speed of change, diversity and urgency of response come into play. The challenge for all businesses is to find their flexibility, to be able to adapt and respond to change. This challenge to large enterprises is not new; it is over twenty years since the publication of Rosabeth Moss Kanter's book "When Giants learn to Dance". Even in smaller organisations we must look at how to build in the responsiveness and flex-flow thinking that we described in the previous chapter. But we will not build such systems until we have first dealt with unproductive mentalities of free-lunch, perpetual growth and excess of competition over shared interest, all propelled by testosterone-fuelled board-room decision-making.

Thus it is clear that the attitudes described throughout this book as affecting individuals and nations have clear parallels in the business sector. The philosophy of corporate competitiveness with its high failure rates is often treated as demonstrating free-market system success. "Look how the weak and inefficient are being weeded out", is the standard refrain. While this view holds a portion of the truth, we must also recognise that it is not the whole truth. It is often wasteful of both human and material resources. We should remember that the big can use their muscle to crush even high-quality threats, an accusation frequently made against Microsoft as one example.

Since responsiveness and flexibility will be key to the delivery of the manifesto, retaining diversity may be as important to the business world as it is in natural ecosystems. Such agility will be also be central to a form of capitalism which is capable of balancing the interests of all stakeholders in the "multiple bottom lines" models now espoused by many. This kind of thinking is embedded in the SDi approach to organisational design, with principles that reflect the theoretical understandings that enabled Clare W. Graves to foresee our current challenges four decades ago. The changes proposed in international systems and the shifts in our individual perception of money will largely find their means of delivery through the world's many businesses. The corporate perspective is crucial.

How is responsiveness delivered?

It is well-known that large corporations control major proportions of the global economy and that some of the largest are economically larger than many nations. But smaller and medium-sized businesses (SME's) are no less crucial to the change, and face many of the same challenges, and they may have an advantage in their ability to get their arms around the level of change which is required. One UK regional development authority has stated that the UK deficit problem would be eliminated if half of the SME's that fail could be helped to know how to survive.

Following the 2010 election the UK's Public Sector was called upon to re-imagine its structure, processes, function and culture under the banner of delivering the new administration's Big Society / Lean Government agenda. Since then retraining your body while your food intake is being reduced has appeared too much to ask. Or perhaps the demand was simply beyond their capacity from the start. Like them, very few private sector business leaders have faced this kind of change before so it will be quite natural that one response to the requirements presented in the list of goals will be to say that the task is impossible. Many who say this will believe it strongly to be true; others will either want it to be true, or will pretend it is true because they are daunted and insecure about the challenge it represents.

It is not the function of this book to describe all the techniques involved, but it is important that we make it known that they exist. The outlines of the approach can be seen in documents on my website at www.spiralfutures.com where I present them under the heading of "Simplexity". Simplexity is the simplicity that reveals itself when you raise yourself to a higher perspective above complexity. Barrett Brown's white paper[xiv] "The Future of Leadership for Conscious Capitalism covers this conceptual area, as does Richard Barrett's book "The Values-driven Organisation".

The road to self-organisation

Mentioned earlier, Frederic Laloux in his book "Reinventing Organisations" has described what happens when companies become self-organising. Self-organisation is a characteristic which connects organisational life to the root concept that it is, or should be, organic in the way that our bodily metaphors indicated in the previous chapter. Laloux gives insight into the ways that we can remove controls and constraints to enable this. Such transformations require new viewpoints on the nature of change and readiness for it. Some of the change involves taking components that have been used elsewhere and assembling them into appropriate packages. Other aspects require a shift in focus, articulating goals in new ways that will align systems to those new targets and elicit different actions. Perhaps most crucially, the ways that we structure, control and lead organisations and teams will need to shift. We can align people to their roles in different ways than before with awareness of their Values, and how these fit together.

The shift out of linear thinking which was described in the previous chapter has the capability to free up resources, increase the fit of individuals to roles and to decentralise the intelligence and decision-making so that the organisation has the organic and adaptive responsiveness to engage successfully with a complex, fast-changing world. As mentioned above it was recognised two decades ago that giants must learn to dance and many large organisations became as a result less centralised, more diversified, allowing greater autonomy to divisions. In some ways this was a precursor to our current situation, recognition of the central

---

[xiv] https://associates.metaintegral.org/blog/future-leadership-conscious-capitalism

upward dynamic in the spiral and the core relationship and tension between size and complexity. Our challenge now is that complexity affects all organisations simultaneously because of the pace, diversity, unpredictability, interconnectedness and multi-stakeholder demands.

One of the fears generated by this challenge is that even if it is feasible, such a substantial change to the organisational life will be impossibly expensive and disruptive. It may already be dawning on some businesses that there is a parallel here to the statement once made by the South African Education Minister "If you think education is expensive, try ignorance". The choice to do nothing is going or already gone. But the change does not have to be expensive. Like the postponement of a health-check for a niggling condition it is likely to be less expensive and less disruptively surgical when engaged with early. With time and planning there is greater potential for early return on investment which will fund future stages.

It is a feature of our developmental journey that as we embed the rules and order of stage 4 we become excessively oriented towards the processes themselves. In many areas this has been made worse by the expectations of stage 6 Values, where consumer protection is one of the drivers for quality. From the two stages together, demands for Health and Safety, quality standards and various aspects of respect for humanity are in focus. All are generally positive in intention and can be beneficial in outcome.

However, as in all things there can be imbalance and we are all familiar with the excesses of political correctness or the H&S stupidity which called for children to wear protective helmets under horse-chestnut trees. The road to hell is paved with good intentions. The road is also serviced and maintained by lawyers who use Stage 5 strategies to turn every twist of fate into somebody's legal culpability. The result is often that spurious law-suits are conceded rather than incur the costs of defending them, thereby driving up costs and insurance premiums to the point where some businesses cease to be viable.

Whether from quality systems, government compliance or human protection both real and spurious, the result has been that process and procedure has become a huge overhead to many organisations. Perhaps worse, it has affected

142

the way we think, the targets we pursue and the way in which we measure success. There is some truth in the belief that if you can't measure what you are doing, you can't change it; at the same time, it is critical to measure the right things. Spurious measurement, one-dimensional focus and poor relationship with the outcomes that really matter are all frequent side-effects of the process culture. If we are to create flexibility we have to undo the tick-box mentality without damaging compliance, quality, common-sense and care. The solution to all of these problems requires a shift in culture away from process and towards outcomes.

Measuring outcomes works

I once had the good fortune to work for two years with a major organisation which transformed itself over that period after their leader set the goal that they must be number one in customer satisfaction surveys for their industry in every quarter for the coming year. Shops, call centres, device manufacture and support systems were all worked on with this goal in mind. All incentives were geared to that achievement. The result was that two years later the company was the most successful and profitable in a very competitive field, a position which it still held two years later. For clarity I must state that this transformation was not driven by SDi methods and it is given as an example of outcome-oriented management but I would also assess that at that time the company in question provided a good example of "second-tier" management thinking.

In a 2014 presentation to the UK Chapter of Conscious Capitalism, Sudhakar Ram[xv], CEO of systems provider Mastek described a more complete transition that is underway in his organisation. Included in their shift is that they are abandoning traditional ways of budgeting, goal-setting, appraisals, distributing these and the associated accountability to the teams themselves. They are moving away from financial metrics in favour of outcomes such as being "an admired company". They have reduced central control as much as possible within legal limits and in many areas have no policies. If self-accountability

---

[xv] Cited earlier as author of "The Connected Age"

fails this would be managed by exception. The results in the early days of this journey indicate increased engagement from employees who come up with ideas that are above what was demanded of them, and enthusiasm from clients who feel even more engaged. 90% of Mastek's business is with existing customers so there are also bottom-line benefits in reduced selling costs.

The shift that has been described throughout this book is a long-term change. It encompasses major strategic goals, re-alignment of processes and shifts in leadership style, management structure and behavioural culture. Such a long-term focus may seem to be unsupportive to short-term flexibility and responsiveness. But the image of transformation is a little like dealing with obesity. It would take exercise, diet and training to produce a ballet dancer from within that excess and is not accomplished at a stroke. Once achieved however, the flexibility is lasting.

No one-size solutions

For each part of the change, techniques are available and the choice of approach will vary by organisation, and even by department. The change in leadership style will differ in respect of individual managers. The reason for this is that the Values systems currently in place dictate what the natural next step must be. The shift from Stage 4 to Stage 5 is a different transformation from that required to move from Stage 5 to Stage 6. There is no pre-determined outcome and no standard journey.

Likewise, different functions benefit from different Values balances. Accounting and engineering functions will be different from marketing and sales. Much can be achieved by improving the fit of individuals to roles, and significant benefits derived from relatively small changes. The toolkits to be used are very likely to already exist, but the art is in knowing which of them (if any) needs to be applied. It is also possible that many parts of the organisation are alright as they are, and important to know when to leave things well alone. Thus the package of measures will always be tailored, but because of this they will not waste effort. It is in the nature of Spiral Dynamics that beneath the complexity is an elegant simplicity, once the approach is understood.

Throughout this book we have repeated the refrain of complexity resulting from urgency, scale and diversity of stakeholders. At every turn, new attitudes to growth, co-operation and control have been called for. The shift from Big Government to smarter and leaner government runs in parallel to a private sector rethink that delivers to the needs of a second tier world. Banks and financial institutions will be called upon to deliver prudence and compliance through cultural realignment as well as through regulation. This is the only way to prevent Stage 5 strategists from out-smarting the slower Stage 4 regulation and is another example of measuring by outcomes rather than by procedure. It has long been understood that ignorance of the law is no excuse. In the future it must be equally self-evident that moral ignorance is also unacceptable. This thinking will apply equally to corporations and small businesses who will be critical to the delivery of a functional world.

None of the above should be taken to imply that all changes will be deliberately engineered. The shift into the new world will happen with the same inevitability as the changes which followed the invention of the printing press, which precipitated a new flow of information and propelled the intellectual and social changes of the enlightenment.

The case for this statement is made in depth by Tapscott and Williams in their book "MacroWikinomics". They cite numerous examples of the way that a new collaborative form is already happening, fuelled both by new thinking and by the technical capabilities of the internet, which they describe as the age of networked intelligence. They describe the new principles for achieving a world that is secure, prosperous, just and sustainable. The principles are Collaboration, Openness, Sharing, Integrity and Interdependence. Spiral Dynamics master Don Beck uses the tagword "DOTS – Connecting what matters to deliver what works in the age of collaboration" to describe a similar world.

It is no accident that the complex problems of existence which arise from our technological acceleration arrive together with the means to solve those problems. Human ingenuity is already making this happen. Google and Wikipedia; collaborative learning models in education; new economic enterprise initiatives; micro-loans (Grameen Bank) and micro-investments (Kiva.org) are showing the way. The Iranian dictatorship's attempt to control information and prevent the organisation of protest was subverted by social networking technologies. Whistle-blowing is now facilitated by WikiLeaks. In the Arab world, bloggers are the new freedom fighters.

Thus much is occurring naturally and we do not have to engineer all change. More will come about when we become skilled, or even simply develop the habit of nurturing contexts in which people self-organise. But corporations risk being left behind if they do not prepare themselves for this new world. The Kaufmann Foundation's analysis of recent U.S. Census bureau data reveals that nearly two-thirds of net new jobs are created by companies less than five years old. Once again, the Conscious Capitalism message is endorsed. Entrepreneurs will lead the recovery. Older companies either adapt to this reality or they will find themselves failing. We are not going back to the old economy. In that sense, as Economist Robert Reich has observed, we can't "recover" and must ask instead how and when the new economy will begin. Arguably it has already begun and our challenge is to support and propel the transition.

All of these trends will increase the opportunity for each of us to make a difference. Wherever we live and work, city or village, business or public sector, we will have more influence as collaborations become the norm of local delivery. This increases the requirement for all of us to become conscious of the effects of our choices and actions. It has been said that most of our law could be replaced by the simple injunction to "be reasonable". It might equally be suggested that this would be made almost complete by the additional requirement to "take care".

The goals that we are shortly to examine call for us to inculcate and demand the conscious application of common sense and to measure success by human and planetary outcomes rather than by compliance. This will root our economic survival in a world which applies "care first" and not "money first" thinking and embeds that care in a systemic balancing of our multiple needs. The goals draw together the strands of our argument for personal and systems change into a whole.

146

Summary Nuggets

For corporations to work in the new environment they too must adopt non-linear approaches.

Management by outcomes will increasingly replace management by process.

There will also be a shift towards self-accountability, towards soft and subjective assessment and away from purely mechanical or financial measurements.

Compliance assessment will depend less on doing the right thing and more on delivering the right result.

Corporations will need to become increasingly self-organising and less centrally controlled in order to respond directly to stakeholder needs, and deliver local or niche knowledge in its arenas of expertise.

Section 4: Co-creating our future

We must build the foundations of tomorrow's prosperity by expanding the focus of accounting and reporting from financial and manufactured forms of capital (for example, infrastructures, buildings, and equipment) to embrace other forms, including intellectual (intellectual property, patents, tacit knowledge, and intangible assets like brands), human (people's competencies, capabilities, and experience), social (shared norms, common values, key stakeholder relationships, and an organization's social license to operate), and natural (air, water, land, minerals, forests, biodiversity, and wider ecosystem health) forms.

John Elkington and Jochen Seitz "The Breakthrough Challenge

14. Shaping the Shift

"Markets could not flourish without a strong underlying moral culture, animated by empathy and fellow-feeling, by our ability to understand our common bond as human beings and to recognize the needs of others."

Adam Smith

How do we support and enable the transition from competition and exploitation into collaboration and mutual sustainability? Others may share my sense of irony that the quote above from Adam Smith, guru of free-market libertarian approaches to the economy, has articulated the essential foundations so clearly. Free markets must be fuelled by care and humanity. As Don Beck would say, *"live and let live is not enough; we must thrive and help thrive"*.

If you were to read articles by economists, exemplified by those that can be found on the website of the right-wing think-tank Adam Smith Institute, you would find a lot of talk about money. You would find arguments about the principles such as how much money the government should be allowed to spend as a percentage of our national income. You would find suggestions for laws such as "thou shalt not borrow more than 3% of GDP in any year". What you would typically not find are articles or statements about people, about how we care for one another. The common bond of human beings and the recognition of needs are absent from their conversation. Smith's moral culture, fellow-feeling and empathy are not included.

Of course economists have one piece of the puzzle. We do need to understand the big picture of how money flows and incorporate it into our solutions. But most economists only understand money. They take a money-first view in which our ills come from getting the money wrong. Get the money right, and life will be rosy, they imply. Hopefully we have already seen beyond these attitudes. In the new world, money will need to <u>follow</u> our human choices, not dictate them.

For sure, this is not easy but it could be easier than we think if we have the collective courage to make the necessary shift. We have seen that humans have

149

a tendency to overbalance into self-centredness and to reach beyond our grasp. We can be and have been, seduced into greed. The suggestion from economists that we might need to put limits on our borrowing are not without common sense. We have to learn to live in present time.

Our task in developing a money system for the future is complex. It has to achieve a multitude of balances. A simple mechanistic model for money is not adequate and this is why it has been failing. As we have seen, one reason for this is that money is dynamic, not static. It has to flow, and the speed of its flow is one of the factors in how well an economic system is functioning. Just looking at numbers does not instantly reveal what needs to be known. It takes perspective and insight to visualise the time dimension and this is often absent. You will not find it in presentations of the budget deficit.

A second challenge is that the numbers may be capable of expressing quantity, but they are not capable of expressing value. Expensive does not necessarily mean better. An original Van Gogh would cost you millions, but it is quite possible to get the same artistic experience, or close enough for most of us, from a really good reproduction. Shopping around may save you 25% on a purchase, but its value to you has not dropped. Of course, this book is a much, much better read if you paid full price for it.

More than anything, we established earlier that the way we use money is in itself an expression of our values. When we desire material reward and the best consumer goods, these desires affect how we view the money they would cost us. In the coming world where planetary survival is almost certainly at stake, money will express a very different set of values. Accordingly, it would be helpful to set out the criteria we might be looking to fulfil with our redesigned money system. What are our values and requirements?

The overview

Said Dawlabani is the leading expert in the value-systems approach to economics. The presentation of human development stages in this book is a high-level overview of how humans have evolved. In his book "Memenomics" Said takes this overview right down to the detail of how the value systems have

150

affected economic cycles. He extends the view of predictability that we gave in Chapter 2 to explain the detail of economic policies, particularly those that reflect stages 3, 4 and 5 viewed through American history since the Civil War. He shows how each stage has risen to its peak and then collapsed as it is superseded by the next.

In the framing of economics he names the stages more explicitly than I have to date. Stage 3 is Fiefdoms of Power, the era of railroads and industrialisation. Stage 4 is Patriotic Prosperity, the era of New Deal economics and the rise in European Social Democracy, taking our economies from post-depression through World War 2 and into the 1960's with the expansion of the middle-class and the strong regulation of the Kennedy Presidency.

The Stage 5 economy rises in the Reagan / Thatcher era fuelled by Milton Friedman's monetarist theories from the 1970's and Said calls it the "only money matters" cycle. Its other keynotes were deregulation and the emphasis on laissez-faire versions of capitalism. We are familiar by now with where this has taken us.

As he describes it, the cycle that reflects stage 5 is the one currently going through its entropy and collapse phase. In his words *"we will see how this cycle came to represent the values of the Strategic Enterprise fifth-level system, which emerged as a higher expression of economic evolution out of a system burdened by antiquated rules and regulations. We can see how finance evolved and became the tail that wagged the dog and how the promise of the post-industrial society was derailed."*

Part 2 of his book is concerned with the search for a new paradigm alongside the recognition that the "predatory value systems are still running the global economy today." Stage 6 and the egalitarian views that it represents, aligned with democratisation of information and deeper human understanding, are at the core of this redesign. So too are the beginnings of knowledge economies and the rise of service industries.

Alongside this, many countries, particularly in Northern Europe, intensified the provision of socialised medicine and care, plus early-years education. In

America too, the years of education extended into College and University for increasing numbers. Significant in this too is the rise of women, whose freedom from the home was powered by Stage 5 industrial creations like the washing machine and made available both the energy for a women's equality movement and for a large rise in the female workforce and two-breadwinner families. Many of the service and care sectors depend on this female workforce. All of these egalitarian outcomes are components of what Said Dawlabani calls "The Democratisation of Information" cycle.

Since both of us have used the Graves/Beck Spiral Dynamics perspective and since both Said and I were exploring money-related topics over the same period it is far from accidental that the sequence above is fully in parallel to the descriptions given so far in this book. I acknowledge again his influence on my thinking. The difference is that Said is looking more from the economic systems perspective where his analysis of the historical trajectory and the political influences goes both wide and deep. My explorations began more in a view through the lens of human ways of thinking and the internal aspects of human values. The outer-world economic realities were reflections of the consciousness that sits beneath such social and political forces. It is time to bring our two perspectives together. The world that we are describing is the same world. The question we are both exploring is "What's next?"

Systemic Integration: The map after Stage 6

In presentations of the Graves/Beck viewpoint so far we have interrupted our story after Stage 6. The map required for the reinvention of capitalism is defined by the emergence of Stages 7 and 8.

Here, our human choices reflect how our life conditions call for us to sustain **all** of the first-tier Values system stages that we outlined in Chapter 2. A second-tier world has to be capable of working in the type of **complexity** that this brings and that we outlined in Chapter 6 - a complexity that is magnified by huge cities, global relationships, diversity of human populations, all of them compounded by speed of change and by urgency of need. Stage 7 is **systemic and integrative**, demanding big-picture views of living systems with structures that are responsive to non-linear change. Our current systems are not. The shift into non-linear ways of thinking and being is a bigger transition than any that humanity has previously made. Clare W. Graves predicted 40 years ago that we humans would find ourselves in this position, which he characterised as a "momentous leap". It is just one sign of the strength of the theory that it could be so successfully predictive.

This requires a very flexible arena for business and commerce, one where there is inbuilt intelligence, distributed through the system. It cannot be managed from the top down, or under the control of a centralised bureaucracy. It has to be capable of balancing the needs of all stakeholders and caring for all. We cannot live in an "either-or" way of thinking, where there is an imaginary choice between satisfying shareholders and paying workers a living wage or where big supermarkets squeeze suppliers to the bone in the name of a competition to supply the largest number at the cheapest price. We have to step beyond the notion that "fair trade" is a meaningful label. There is trade or there is exploitation. It's that simple.

Our ability to balance the needs of a whole society extends beyond the trading environment. We have been battling for years with the demands of healthcare for all, providing for our elders, delivering free education to every young person, supporting those who are too physically infirm or mentally damaged to work, preventing child abuse, providing meaningful opportunities to those with special needs, reducing violence, drug dependence and criminality. When a society spends over five times as much per person to incarcerate its criminals as to educate its children it is obvious that we are not getting this right. We need to be ensuring that social care goals of all kinds are met. Even before a recession, capacities have been hugely stretched. It is very clear that this will continue to be a major challenge – indeed it is conceivable that the whole paradigm is unworkable in an era of ageing populations. The redesign of this almost certainly sits as a component of reinventing capitalism and dealing with the polarisation of values around what society is and what we wish it to be.

Stage 8. The planetary holism

Newest of all is our discovery that the planet itself is a stakeholder. Disputes continue about whether climate change is entirely caused by carbon dioxide and the greenhouse effect but there is no doubt of the climate instability itself and little doubt that the greenhouse effect is not helping. Nor is there any doubt that the rate of species extinctions has reached levels probably not seen since the meteorite which ended the supremacy of the dinosaurs. The world will survive the loss of the tiger, the panda and the polar bear however much they sadden us. We do not know quite how much damage is being done by the loss of the thousands of species that we don't know about, wouldn't recognise, couldn't name and wouldn't want to cuddle.

What we do know is that for the 3000 species monitored in the Living Planet Index produced collaboratively by the World Wildlife Fund and the London Zoological Society, numbers have declined by 52% in the 40 years to 2014. This figure goes up by a few percent every two years. The Index only deals with vertebrates – creatures with backbones – and does not tell us about insects or other invertebrates. The major causes of change – climate, deforestation, over-fishing, rivers drying up, destruction of other habitats and pollution – are all largely driven by human activity.

We don't know at what point the loss of those species might cause the collapse of an entire ecosystem. So many changes have unforeseen effects, such as the way in which Himalayan glacier loss will affect vast areas of Asian food production. There is also evidence of the benefits of reversing the effects of human interference. Since the re-introduction of wolves into Yellowstone Park there has been continuous improvement to its environment, its support of multiple species and even the health of its river systems.[xvi] Extinctions take away such options. We don't know how close to the edge we may be.

Political consequences

Financial practicalities also affect political outcomes. Whether economic or ecological in origin the threat of starvation or absence of drinking water can cause wars or drive mass migration and political conflict. And even if the

---

[xvi] www.youtube.com/watch?v=ysa5OBhXz-Q

pressures are not so imminently connected to survival, exploitation ultimately breeds resentment. In bygone times, the West had its empires and benefited economically from slavery. Modern transportation frees us from the requirement to relocate slaves. Now we only have to transport the work. Yesterday's slaves are working in today's sweat-shops and may be willing to do so because this represents a step up for them. We cannot expect that to continue indefinitely. As with the factory workers and miners of 100 years ago, inequalities will bring rebellions. They always do.

At the extreme, when food is priced beyond people's means, they will adopt Stage 1 Values and will do whatever is required for survival, including war and revolution. The French revolution started this way and took the top 1% to the guillotine. In the US the current economic pressures are fuelling both anti-islamic sentiment and issues around Mexican border immigration. Such shifts are not merely the potential for history to repeat itself, they are predictable changes based on the dynamics of life conditions and Values systems as seen through the SDi lens. This is not to present a pessimistic view of the future, but to emphasise the importance of our becoming conscious and taking the appropriate actions. Those actions cannot choose between humans and planet. The illusion that such a choice exists has been embedded in our problems and must end.

The transition to a new way with money

Against this background it may seem quite a daunting task to come up with a new money system. It will be the work of many people to devise and build such a system and it is not like a Windows version upgrade – cannot simply be installed at a chosen date and time. There is a transition to be made and the new will have to emerge from the old, preferably without that old system undergoing complete and utter collapse. Some of that transition will come about through our choices – that the mechanisms of the old money system remain in place, but we make strong collective decisions to pull the levers differently, or to have the same bicycle, ridden in a different direction. But that will only buy time to accomplish the remainder of what is required.

All the economic proposals being made in the mainstream of econo-politics assume that the future can be achieved solely by making adjustments within the existing system. As stated, that is a "deckchairs on the Titanic" exercise which I believe we have already discredited. Even so, what follows here is not a complete new design, offered ready and working. I am not that clever and have not encountered anyone else who is. Instead, the intention here is to present a set of Values to work from, criteria to satisfy and goals to aim for. By articulating those goals it is to be hoped that we can see the overarching picture of what is needed, what has to emerge and what our collective creativity must bring about.

Many excellent and promising suggestions have already been made which could help us find our way to those goals. There are many people who have pieces of this puzzle ready to assemble. There are many who recognised that their piece must slot in with others. So far we do not seem to have the table to put the puzzle on. There are many groupings arising to support the essential conversations and collaborations. Most of these like Conscious Capitalism have focussed from within businesses and organisations and for good reason. Businesses are likely to be the engine of change. However I suggest we are already seeing that they are not enough. The system itself must support and align with their changes. Wider cars need wider roads. I hope that what follows may help the necessary collaborations to coalesce further so as to reach the critical mass which affects how governments think.

Throughout what follows please remember that this is not just something for "them" to do. Underneath the change in financial systems there will have to be the changes in our thinking. Above or beneath all, is a shift in our consciousness, our individual steps out of fear, greed, control, power and survival. That's you and me folks! "They" can't do it but WE can and we must.

The inner and the outer

The next chapter presents the list of manifesto items. In it you will see changes that we must make on the inside, shifts in how we individually think and react. These individual changes naturally accumulate in how we think and respond collectively. That collective response shows up in our newspapers and TV. It

156

is visible in our radio shows and in the commentaries that we accept and foster in our presenters. Some of the presenters make their living because we will buy into their fear-and-anger points of view. We will need more alternatives to those presentations, more outlets that support the many who know better. And more of us will be needed who will take the time and make the effort to talk back. Much of what we are dealing with is not lack of intellectual intelligence, but the damage done when it lacks accompanying emotional intelligence. Individual responses don't only arrive in the collective; they are influenced by it. Changing that influence requires our action.

Central to our message is the theme that what we think and how we think shows up in our individual and collective choices and behaviours. That does not go beyond conventional wisdom. Less conventional is the recognition that we build our systems to enable and support those choices. We shape our world accordingly. Our Values systems in stages 4, 5 and 6 all show up in the outer world. For example, Stage 4 ordering produced our accounting and our engineering. Stage 5 produced our high-powered banking and financial systems and the huge technological underpinnings. Stage 6 produced our welfare systems, elder support and socialised medical support.

All of these stages of thinking define what is possible in the world. They are so strongly built in to the structures of our world that we tend to view them as "given" as if they are part of natural law, the "way things are". This is not the case. In nearly all cases there are alternatives. Much of the next chapter consists of the outer changes and these may well seem more difficult than the inner ones. These structures and Values need to be looked at as a collective. Taken piecemeal they are likely to seem unachievable because they are a system. They work together. In a system, changing one component can be undesirable, bringing instability and collapse. You need to see the whole of what follows before attempting to critique a single piece.

This is not to say that these suggestions are beyond criticism; of course they are not and I am certain that they will be improved upon and added to. At the same time they need to be addressed together as well as individually. A natural design evolves its own checks and balances. Since this is not a natural design but a human construction we must emulate natural design as well as we are able and also be willing to adjust the balances as we go. We will learn from the changes we introduce and must not regard our lessons as failures. The design cannot be perfect and even as it is introduced, the conditions it must deal with will change. Since the current system is self-evidently very imperfect we need to start changes as soon as possible. We must therefore not judge it by the standard "is it perfect?" or we will never find the courage to change. The questions are rather "Will this result in progressive improvement?" and "Will it be in alignment with the new Values that we aspire to?"

Lastly before viewing the list please do not see the order of presentation as representing priorities. That would be inappropriate both for the reasons of systemic connectedness just given and because the priorities will be determined by a combination of what is most urgently needed, what is most achievable without causing instability, what can we most easily get agreement on and what can be done with the resources we can bring. In relation to resources however please also be aware that what we currently think we can bring is conditioned by our view of what is critical. When we perceive military threats we mobilise huge resources; you need only to look at what happened to economies in World War 2 as energy was diverted into the war effort. What can we do and what will we do when we believe that our economic reality is the greatest danger we face?

Summary Nuggets

Stage 7 of human evolution calls for systemic, flexible and integrative systems that deliver increased functionality.

Stage 8 of human societal evolution demands an increase in planetary holism – not just the recognition of our systemic dependence for survival on the planet as a resource-base, but the nature of interdependence in a web of existence.

Our new money systems will need to reflect and facilitate these relationships.

The new systems must provide coherent and integrated changes at the individual, corporate, societal and global levels.

Our perspectives on societal change will need to recognise the relationship between our inner systems – how we think – and our outer systems – how we structure the things and processes to facilitate changes in how we think.

Our goals will need to match the multi-dimensional and interactive nature of the world that we are seeking to improve.

15. Goals for a new capitalism

We are not all guilty but we are responsible

Lawrence Bloom

Inner goals

1) **Money must mean something.** Our thinking must support a close connection between the money we use and the physical realities that it ascribes monetary value to.

2) **Money cannot be created out of nothing.** We must purge ourselves of any ideas which encourage any belief that money can be created out of nothing or that it can grow by itself, without other creative action

3) **Be grounded in the present.** We need a way of being that helps us to live in the present. Where we borrow from our personal or collective future we are assisted to stay grounded and discouraged from over-reaching. We look for "paying it forward" approaches in real terms and find modern equivalents of the Amish community barn-raising day. Where we look to the future, we look at how to build for that in the present.

4) **Eliminate the throwaway mentality.** We cannot live successfully in the belief that everything in our world is somehow dispensable.

5) **Build our awareness of interdependence.** Our thinking and Values must increasingly recognise the global and local interdependence of all human beings. It must then extend to a recognition of our dependence on ecosystems and of the impact that human decisions have on them.

6) **Allow reward for creativity and inspiration.** We can and should encourage individuals and groups to excel, to be creative and to receive abundantly from the fruits of their inspiration, their hard work, their

investment in research, their dedication in building businesses and their willingness to take risks. Fairness cannot be achieved and is not to be achieved by suppressing the individual spirit

7) **Support the flow of wealth.** We must encourage and incentivise those who are creating personal surplus so as to discourage hoarding, support the free flow of money, propel investment in each other; that we value giving and foster relationship

8) **Balancing stakeholder needs**. This is fundamental to Conscious Capitalism and its many similars. We require corporate cultures that are capable of meeting the needs of all stakeholders in a balanced way, where shareholder profit exists alongside customer service, supplier relationship, employee well-being, pension funding, social responsibility, regulatory compliance, local and planetary sustainability. It requires us to place value on trust and happiness in the same way that we do for brand loyalty, and to recognise the negative value of ecological damage.

9) **Gifting and Receiving.** We must improve our awareness and understanding of what these mean, how they contribute to each other and how we live in balance

10) **Freedom and Responsibility.** We must improve our education, awareness and understanding of the necessary balance in these internal dynamics.

11) **Collaboration and Competition.** We must re-educate and improve awareness of the falsehoods erected around Darwinism and increase the recognition that evolution and ecology are a dynamic balance of competitive and mutually supportive linkages.

Systems Intelligence: Outer goals

12) **Money must mean something.** Our systems must support a close connection between the money we use and the physical realities that it ascribes monetary value to.

161

13) **Money cannot be created out of nothing.** Our systems must discourage activity based on the belief that money can be created out of nothing or that it can grow by itself, without other creative action. This includes reversing of the policy by which banks are now in effect printing money through the issue of unrestricted debt.

14) **Short-termism is destructive.** Our systems must encourage long-term investment and discourage short-term speculative manipulation (this to include further evaluation of the "Tobin tax" or similar mechanisms). The balance of stock-market behaviour needs to favour investment over trading and to make it difficult for investment managers to profit from unnecessary "churn" of client funds.

15) **Inhibit currency speculation.** The buying and selling of currencies should be directly connected with the functional use of the money and currency speculation and manipulation should be strongly inhibited

16) **Align compensation with long-term performance.** Many inner goals and cultural change impulses will be undermined if the external systems reward individuals for short-termism

17) **A level playing field.** We need increasingly to recognise the life conditions of different peoples, cultures and regions, assist them to manage their own development and avoid exploitation arising from the differences between our conditions and theirs

18) **Balancing stakeholder needs.** We must create supportive legal, governance and financial frameworks to enable corporate cultures to more easily meet the needs of all stakeholders in a balanced way. (See no. 8 above).

19) **Simultaneous Policy and global co-ordination.** Find ways to co-ordinate global policy-making which are effective in countering national self-interest, recognise interdependency and which better balance the collaborative and competitive aspects of economic behaviour

20) **Costs and benefits are not all material.** We must develop the capability to recognise and assess costs and benefits at both material and non-material levels

Connecting Values, goals and monetary value

21) **Living systems have Value.** We must extend our ability to ascribe monetary value in a way that encompasses living systems – that it is assumed that every species and ecosystem has financial worth even where we have not yet discovered it or measured it in human terms

22) **The environment has Value.** We must improve our systems for recognising the financial cost of environmental impact, extending beyond toxicity, atmospheric and habitat damage to include the sensed aspect of contribution to our quality of life and that of future generations

23) **True Cost Accounting.** We must not continue to externalise costs to be left unpaid or picked up at random by others and by society. Our financial thinking about the cost of goods must recognise fully not only the cost of manufacture, but the cost of packaging, package disposal, recycling, the economics of repair and non-repair. We must account for cost of final disposal where we fail in those others.

24) **Full Cost raw materials recognition.** Enhance our financial thinking and systems to recognise the true cost of raw materials – the environmental costs of obtaining them, the impact on inhabitants of source regions, the cost of proper management of toxic wastes from refining them and the subsequent recovery of exploited areas

25) **Planetary stewardship.** Develop systems which ensure and enforce that ownership of, control over or material benefit from any natural planetary resource is closely coupled with its stewardship; recognising that none of us own the Earth or its riches, that we are at best co-tenants and joint beneficiaries

26) **True National Benefit assessment.** We need to replace monetary measures of national success (such as GDP) with measurement that also assesses physical health, social, cultural and spiritual well-being, community strength and cohesion, habitat quality, human longevity and systemic sustainability

27) **True National Cost recognition.** We require the ability to distinguish economically between activities which are productive (such as agriculture and manufacture) and activities which however essential represent human costs such courts, prisons, hospitals, social care, waste management and insurance claims   We must measure both Gross Domestic Product and Gross Domestic "Cost".

28) **Improve our thinking around inflation and growth.** We must reduce systems and activities which embed monetary inflation as an inevitable feature of economic life and assume that our children and grandchildren will pick up the bill. This requires us to learn to distinguish natural and systemic planetary growth from the growth of money supply

29) **Corporate stewardship.** Treat shareholders as suppliers of capital rather than as owners of the enterprise and require that their attitude to the corporation is one of long-term stewardship

30) **Corporate legal responsibility.** Corporations are not persons. They must not be treated legally as if they have equivalent rights to individual humans.

31) **Preventive thinking.** We require increased ability to distinguish and assign value to costs incurred (investments in quality) which inhibit later costs; for example between health systems to treat sickness and health systems to maintain wellness. It may not serve society to have prisons that run for profit, where companies benefit from higher crime figures. How do we create a peace industry to balance the armaments one? For the sake of our children we must require governments to enumerate and be accountable for consequences beyond their term of office.

32) **Governmental long-term responsibilities**. For the sake of ourselves and our children we must require governments to enumerate and be accountable for consequences of their decisions beyond their term of office.

33) **Recognising societal benefit.** We need to move away from the simple division between "for profit" and "not-for-profit" activities, reducing the discrepancies in value assigned between those who work for the benefit of others and those who work to gain benefit from others. We must reduce the devaluation of the former and the change way that teachers, nurses and social carers are viewed only as a cost to society.

34) **Balance Freedom and Responsibility**   Improve our societal capacity to tell the difference between the inalienable value of individual freedom and the right to be socially, environmentally or even self-destructive.

35) **Socially responsible valuing of risk.** Create systems which direct the human impulse to gamble and to play with risk towards productive outcomes and away from destructive ones

36) **Right-scale Distributed Democracy.** We need to improve the balance between centralised and locally accountable decision-making, which in most Western countries is over-centralised. This will increase relevance of decisions, productive economy, closer attention to cost management and increased engagement with the democratic process.

I should note here that there is no explicit mention of ethics in this list. I would like however to mention the work of Roger Steare in his book "Ethicability" and his "Moral DNA" profiling system. My view is that ethics runs through this list. Having a goal that we should "think and behave ethically" somehow manages to be simultaneously too obvious, too essential and also redundant.   Roger Steare's very practical approach maps very well to the interplay of stage 4,5 and 6 viewpoints, but I make no claim that he endorses this perception.

There is also no mention of the way that we relate money and work. I was tempted to include the proposal for "basic income", a system of unconditional income for every citizen. This is too complex to discuss here will have different impacts from country to country and its benefits / downsides highly dependent on how it would be delivered. My personal belief is that in Western countries it would offer a great deal. The evidence suggests that any assumption that it encourages idleness is incorrect. There are many potential gains in preventing societal costs, including crime and health and it is not only the socialised economies of Western Europe that would see benefits. It could work for the USA too.

The bottom line of all these propositions is that we must rebalance, that we have to wrest control from the system where money makes the rules, replacing it with ones where human beings and human values are in charge of the rules. Life is not equal. These changes do not prevent the existence of rich people or of themselves avoid there being poor people. Individuals will have their free choice, their destiny and their portion of life's good or bad fortune. At the moment however, those who have more money gain more than merely the choices that it offers them in their own lives. Money will always bring "power to…" and those who have been successful or fortunate are entitled to manage their own lives. At the moment money also gives people the levers of power, in the form of "power over….". They disproportionately determine how the world will operate for others.

As we shift the way that money works we shift the balances away from money making the rules towards human beings making the rules. This develops our capacity individually and collectively to care for ourselves, for each other and the Earth, which all cultures that have not become disconnected from her acknowledge as the Mother, the source of our life and our nourishment.

16. Understanding the goals: Connecting the dots

If a man runs after money, he's money-mad; if he keeps it he's a capitalist; if he spends it he's a playboy; if he doesn't get it he's a ne'er do well; if he doesn't try to get it he lacks ambition. If he gets it without working for it he's a parasite; and if he accumulates it after a lifetime of hard work, people call him a fool who never got anything out of life.

Vic Oliver

Some of the items in the list of goals have been thoroughly covered by our analysis of the current system and some are hopefully self-evident. Others are worthy of some further explanation or analysis.

Emotional and Spiritual Intelligence: The Inner goals

1) **Money must mean something.** Our thinking must support a close connection between the money we use and the physical realities that it ascribes monetary value to.

2) **Money cannot be created out of nothing.** We must purge ourselves of any ideas which encourage any belief that money can be created out of nothing or that it can grow by itself, without other creative action

3) **Be grounded in the present.** We need a way of being that helps us to live in the present. Where we borrow from our personal or collective future we are assisted to stay grounded and discouraged from over-reaching. We look for "paying it forward" approaches in real terms and find modern equivalents of the Amish community barn-raising day. Where we look to the future we should look at how to build for that in the present.

Time and your busted pensions

We have dealt extensively with the way that money distorts time. It is possibly our most important message about fear and greed and their relationship to debt.

But we have not dealt to the same extent with savings and pensions, nor with the impact of pure giving.

In a stable system with relative freedom from inflation it is sensible and beneficial to put money aside for a rainy day. I might not want to take the risk of "investing". I might want access to my capital for emergencies. I can stuff my mattress with notes, bury gold bricks in my garden or, if desperate, entrust it to a bank. I can keep it for a short time or a long one, saving it for my child's wedding day or as a deposit for her first house. This behaviour is the opposite of the fearful and greedy over-reaching. Rather than sell my future, I store my past. In times past the banking system helped to keep humanity balanced by maintaining the overall relationship between saving and borrowing.

Pensions are an extension of this system, since they encourage us to put by some of our history for the very long term, against the time when we are no longer fit to work, or better still, able to enjoy the fruits of our productivity in our retirement. A traditional society maintains its elders from the communal production. It values them for their accumulated experience and insight, their stabilising awareness of traditional values and with luck, even wisdom.

When the state pension was thought of, this principle could still apply in a monetary form. The population would expand such that those who are still productive could support those whose productivity was declining. Now this situation is reversing. Lowering birth-rates, coupled with the post-war baby boom, earlier retirement ages and longer life-spans has mean that the state no longer knows where the money will come from in ten years time. Already you will have heard the warnings that retirement ages must rise. I cannot retire at the same age my grandfather did. The increasing dangers of expensive long-term dependency from non-fatal mental or physical incapacity add to this problem.

To counter the effects of this change in population balance and life-expectancy there is an increasing requirement for us to put by money for ourselves. As with savings, inflation is destructive to this process. The money I put by today is not guaranteed to be worth enough. Only if that inflation reflects steady growth in real terms, can my investments out-run it.   Since economies are shown in practice to have long-term cycles, we cannot expect this to work consistently.

Let's look at this simplistically. Let's assume I have a 40-year working life and a 20-year retirement. At the same spending, that would mean I need to put by half of my income during those 40 years to fund my old age. Fortunately, most people need less to live on when retired, being past the time of acquisition and child-rearing. If I can reduce my outgoings by the time I retire to an average of half those that applied while I worked, I would need to create and save a surplus equivalent to a quarter of my outgoings throughout that period in order to fund my pension fully. The reality is that few of us can do even that.

Many have been helped by company pension schemes in larger companies. Governments may support these by allowing contributions to come out of pre-tax income. That may make 5% or 10% of your wage worth 7% or 14% compared with your take-home pay. But it still is not 25%. In the public sector the government has been committed to funding employee pensions, often offering sweeter deals in the past to compensate for low wages. Stakeholder pensions are now on offer to everyone. But none of them can guarantee to beat the system. Intentions that money put by early in an employee's life would grow so as to fund their retirement rely on the assumption that over the decades, investments can beat inflation. There is no guarantee of this, and a major recession (even worse a double-dip) will make a serious mess of such plans. A recent report by accountants KPMG states that one-third of the UK's top 100 companies cannot currently fund their pension commitments and require remedial action.

Even the belief that this growth mechanism can work has aspects of "free lunch" thinking. Many people on retirement annuities or approaching retirement age are finding this out the hard way. Even before the crunch many people were concerned that the money theoretically "put by" in the US Social Security pot has actually been borrowed and spent. Their Government Accountability Office projects that just the costs of maintaining Medicare and social security, on their own, will surpass total tax revenues. Their estimate is that the shortfall will be $40 trillion over the next 75 years. Other countries assume that future taxation will cover the need. None of these systems are sound, particularly if your retirees are part of the baby boom and those destined to pay the taxes are a part of a low-reproduction era. Similarly, the UK Public sector shortfall is now believed to approach £1 trillion.

If none of these thoughts scare you enough, consider the report in the New York Times, 14th June 2010 on New York's State Pension Scheme. States have previously borrowed by selling municipal bonds to investors in order to make their contribution to employee pensions schemes, expecting to pay the bonds off through fund growth. During the crunch, the growth didn't happen. They've come up short. They can't borrow from the capital markets again through a bond issue so they have come up with a wizard wheeze. They propose to borrow the money to fund their contributions to the New York State Pension Fund from .... The New York State Pension Fund. That's right, you take previously saved money out of the fund and then you put it back in as today's savings. And since you have borrowed it, you still owe it and will have to pay it later, plus any administrative costs and interest / inflation effects of course. (Any State employees should now pretend that they didn't read this paragraph.) This is very much like funding your personal pension from your credit card.

4) **Eliminate the throwaway mentality.** We cannot live successfully in the belief that everything in our world is somehow dispensable.

5) **Build our awareness of interdependence.** Our thinking and Values must increasingly recognise the global and local interdependence of all human beings. It must then extend to a recognition of our dependence on ecosystems and of the impact that human decisions have on them.

6) **Allow reward for creativity and inspiration.** We can and should encourage individuals and groups to excel, to be creative and to receive abundantly from the fruits of their inspiration, their hard work, their investment in research, their dedication in building businesses and their willingness to take risks. Fairness cannot be achieved and is not to be achieved by suppressing the individual spirit.

Most societies struggle with fairness and some have oscillated between polarised points of view about how much people should earn, and how heavily and in what way high-wealth individuals should be taxed. This debate is a built in alternation of I and We impulses in successive stages in the spiral.

A second tier viewpoint tells us of the need to harmonise all the preceding stages. In practice, nearly all citizens are willing to accommodate to a balance. We may all complain that the balance is not as we would choose but we accept the consequences of living together in a society.

The purpose of this goal is to make it clear that we must manage this. We do not accept that there is an option which penalises entrepreneurial spirit without doing damage to our collective future. Resentment of success is as damaging as greed.

7) **Support the flow of wealth.** We must encourage and incentivise those who are creating personal surplus so as to discourage hoarding, support the free flow of money, propel investment in each other so that we value giving and foster relationship.

In counterbalance to goal 6, this one acknowledges that the economy thrives on flow and that it should be put to productive use. It does not say how this should be done. The aristocrats of the past created employment for many people. Without the personal choices of wealthy people Mozart would have starved and we would not have the Taj Mahal. Governments rarely create great art or architecture. Without personal philanthropy we would rely on governments to recognise and deal with unmet needs. They are not always good at this. At every level we should support the individual freedom of how people use their money. All that matters to the monetary ecosystem is that money should flow. It doesn't matter whether it flows through artists, temple-builders, social workers or industrial manufacture.

8) **Balancing stakeholder needs.** This is fundamental to Conscious Capitalism and its many equivalents. We require corporate cultures that are capable of meeting the needs of all stakeholders in a balanced way,

where shareholder profit exists alongside customer service, supplier relationship, employee well-being, pension funding, social responsibility, regulatory compliance, local and planetary sustainability. It requires us to place value on trust and happiness in the same way that we do for brand loyalty, and to recognise the negative value of ecological damage.

The reasons why this is essential and the extent of its benefits are at the heart of new business. They are well-laid out in John Mackey's Conscious Capitalism, in Raj Sisodia's Firms of Endearment, in Sudhakar Ram's Connected Age and by many other such thinkers more of whom appear below. The multiple bottom line thinking is gaining wide acceptance. This list is an attempt to expand our awareness of those multiple strands beyond the typical three of "People, Profit and Planet" and to extend their implications beyond the corporate realm and into the economic system as a whole.

9) **Gifting and Receiving.** We must improve our awareness and understanding of what these mean, how they contribute to each other and how we live in balance.

We have become accustomed to the phrase "Give and Take". This is a distortion of how most people live and an insult to all but a very few. Giving is natural to humans. When it ceases to be so this is because our nature is being bent out of shape by fear and greed etc. Healthy humans are not takers either; taking is another effect of these negative emotions.

It would also be natural for healthy humans to receive graciously and with appreciation but many are taught that it is more blessed to give than to receive. That has to be nonsense since giving in the absence of receiving would be an imposition or an abuse. Economic flow requires energetically, financially, emotionally and spiritually that we increase our capacity to receive and gift in equal measure.

10) **Freedom and Responsibility.** We must improve our education, awareness and understanding of the necessary balance in these internal dynamics

This is an aspect of the oscillation between the I and the We in our human thinking and our systems. It has been distorted because the We-oriented Values in stages 2, 4 and 6 have swung towards compulsion and often towards over-constraint. The hierarchies of stages 2 and 4 and the group-think of stage 6 do not completely favour personal responsibility. This brings a reactive response in stages 3 and 5 that overbalances towards free-will. Freedom becomes paramount. A Stage 7 solution must encourage responsibility from within so that I express my individual freedom in my choice to be responsible.

11) **Collaboration and Competition.** We must re-educate and improve awareness of the falsehoods erected around Darwinism and increase the recognition that evolution and ecology are a dynamic balance of competitive and mutually supportive linkages.

The explanation for this goal was given in Chapter 5 when we discussed the misapplication and misunderstanding of Darwin and Malthus. The re-education that is required extends beyond social and economic theories. It is fundamental to errors in scientific thinking too.[xvii]

Systems Intelligence: Outer goals

12) **Money must mean something.** Our systems must support a close connection between the money we use and the physical realities that it ascribes monetary value to.

[xvii] See "The Science of Possibility": Patterns of Connected Consciousness by Jon Freeman and Juliana Freeman. www.scienceofpossibility.net

As described earlier, money is conceptual. It is only real to the extent that it truly represents something more tangible. When we abandoned the gold standard we let go of the last tether. Our view of what is tangible has changed since then. In a knowledge economy we may need to expand our view of what may have a monetary value. But the money itself must have some sort of anchor or it means nothing at all and represents no reality whatsoever. There are suggestions for how this might be achieved such as relating it to a basket of commodities. Said Dawlabani has proposed that we could find a basic measure of productive output – which presumably be one which excludes all which is speculative, artificial, government-printed, debt-fuelled and even service-related but in accordance with our opening chapters measures things which would remain if all the money vanished. Almost any sensible proposal would be an improvement on a hot air balloon with no ballast and no pilot.

In his book "The Death of Money", James Rickards offers strong arguments for the replacement of the gold standard. While he does not accept that the arguments for removing the gold standard are valid, he favours a larger and more flexible system. I recommend his book if you are inquisitive about the arguments which are too detailed and too technical for this space. In addition to arguing for Gold, he also presents the possible position that could be taken by the International Monetary Fund (IMF), and titles his chapter "The Central Bank of the World".

The IMF has its own quasi-currency, the SDR (Special Drawing Right) which represents money given to it by fund member countries and which it can deploy to support economies in trouble. It was a major lender to Ireland, Portugal, Cyprus and Greece post-crash and also has given major support to Mexico and Poland.

While its history is to have been (in his words) "a rich nation's club, lending to support those nation's economic interests" it has the potential to be more than this. It has had its own agenda, which it revealed in a 2011 study, which consists of a plan over years and in several steps to position the SDR as the leading global reserve asset. Within this it plans to reduce the SDR's weighting towards the dollar and increase the influence of other currencies including the Chinese Yuan. It's study concludes "if there were political willingness to do so, these securities could constitute an embryo of global currency."

Rickards states (P.234) that "A well-designed gold standard could work smoothly if the political will existed to enact it and adhere to its noninflationary principles". He further suggest that it would have several possible designs, but his proposal, in order to reduce some of the restrictions perceived to apply to the old gold standard, is to use the SDR as an intermediary, making it into a gold-backed standard, which then holds the value relationships between existing national currencies. While not the global currency proposed by Keynes at Bretton Woods, it would be a partial step in that direction.

13) **Money cannot be created out of nothing.** Our systems must discourage activity based on the belief that money can be created out of nothing or that it can grow by itself, without other creative action. This includes reversing of the policy by which banks are now in effect printing money through the issue of unrestricted debt.

Bubbles, scams both legal and illegal, spurious financial instruments and money unrelated to currency are all causing instability. Some doors should be closed completely. Other areas require much tighter control and regulation This might be based on the concept that if it is not transparent where the money is going, not possible to count where it has gone and we can't maintain track of its ongoing value then it should not be permitted.

14) **Short-termism is destructive. O**ur systems must encourage long-term investment and discourage short-term speculative manipulation (this to include further evaluation of the "Tobin tax" or similar mechanisms). The balance of stock-market behaviour needs to favour investment over trading and to make it difficult for investment managers to profit from unnecessary "churn" of client funds.

15) **Inhibit currency speculation.** The buying and selling of currencies should be directly connected with the functional use of the money and currency speculation and manipulation should be strongly inhibited

The myth of the free market and the damage of speculation We can look at the two goals above in the same light. The free market concept was birthed at a time when people made the decisions themselves. There really was a marketplace, even if it has never been truly free because there have always been monopolistic practices. There have been benefits to larger organisations from economies of scale which brought with their size the ability also to control and manipulate the market. Fernand Braudel[xviii] has documented these forces as far back as the thirteenth century. The full picture of the dynamics are described in Manuel de Landa's "A thousand years of non-linear history"[xix]. The bottom line is that we should stop pretending that there is or has ever been a truly free market.

Even so, whatever a free market might have been or intended to be, those intentions were founded on trade. Transactions took place in human time and were in large measure open to human visibility. If a commodity was warehoused speculatively to await a price rise, people tended to know. This is very different from electronic trading made by computers and betting second by second or hour by hour on the movements of stocks, commodities and currencies. Now you and I can indulge in this and there are many people who offer to train us to do so.

None of this is investment. You will quite likely have heard reference in news bulletins to difficulties caused by "speculation". You may not have

---

[xviii] Fernand Braudel. "The Wheels of Commerce". ISBN: 978-1842-12288-4 Out of print but easily obtainable

[xix] Manuel de Landa 1997. " A thousand years of nonlinear history. ISBN 978-09422-9932-8

had much idea how this works or why it is damaging. What's the difference between the two?

The system was originally constructed to allow those who had money to spare or who wished to save for their future, to lend that money to others in order that they could create something. If your neighbour wanted to start a business, you could lend him the money to do so. The idea of shares in a company is an extension of this principle, where your neighbour sells several people including you a share of that enterprise which you can in turn sell.

Similarly, the system supports you to buy currencies other than the one you use at home. You might want to travel, to buy a house in the sun or to invest in a venture overseas. But as you know, when a country has a successful economy its currency is worth more, and vice versa. Your house in the sun might not rise in value in its own market but if the currency you own it in gains in value you could still make a profit when you sell.

The scenarios above describe choices to buy things largely because of their intrinsic value. In the above example, the gain made from currency fluctuation is a side-effect. But there are other potential reasons for buying. If you know that a company is ripe for takeover, you might buy its shares, speculating on the likely rise in value when it becomes a target. If you believe that another currency is likely to rise in value (or yours to fall) you might put your money into that and wait for the change to deliver a profit. This is where our actions shift into "speculation". It is another example of trying to use money to make more money.

It is also possible to speculate on failure. With shares, the system allows you to promise to sell shares in the future that you do not yet own. You might speculate that a company will lose value and agree to sell it at today's price for delivery in three months, expecting to buy the shares for less before handing them over. This is called "selling short", and similar mechanisms are available for currency. The benefit of this system is that it allows the market to assess and signal the future value of a company, and for those with good judgement to make money from farsightedness. It sends a signal to company management regarding the view that others hold of them. Short-selling can also prevent the price from rising too high, which may protect other potential investors from loss.

The downsides of short-selling are first that the transaction pits one investor against another – it does not contribute to the value of the underlying investment. It is a form of gambling. The bigger negative potential is that people with very large amounts of capital can collude (intentionally or otherwise) to cause instability. They can influence the market and manipulate the price fall to start, undermining market confidence and creating the price slide that they will later profit from. There are plenty of examples.

At root, there are investments which are based on actual assessments of how a company or country will perform. These generally have to be justified by knowledge of its performance and its marketplace, based on publicly available information. That market is necessary, can be regulated for fairness and probity and is generally beneficial.

Alternatively there are investments based on speculating how other investors will react to circumstances. This comes closer to gambling on human behaviour. The second is open to manipulation and can make the operation of the first marketplace unstable, and divorced from actual company performance. At its worst, if the market loses confidence in a company, the rush to sell can drop its price to the extent that it has insufficient assets to trade. Companies and countries alike can be bankrupted. In the case of countries, the market can also effectively force the government to apply policies that are contrary to democratic mandate. When there are multinational corporations whose size exceeds that of a national economy, this allows power and self-interest to reign supreme.

16) **Align compensation with long-term performance.** Many inner goals and cultural change impulses will be undermined if the external systems reward individuals for short-termism.

This goal applies at the level of individual incentive and equally in relation to the activities of investment managers and brokers. Recently Paul Polman, CEO of the large multinational Unilever announced that he would cease issuing quarterly reports because of the way that the market attempted to manipulate his company's value. Richard Branson cites similar reasons for taking Virgin back into private ownership.

17) **A level playing field.** We need increasingly to recognise the life conditions of different peoples, cultures and regions, assist them to manage their own development and avoid exploitation arising from the differences between our conditions and theirs.

18) **Simultaneous Policy and Global co-ordination.** Find ways to co-ordinate global policy-making which are effective in countering national self-interest, recognise interdependency and which better balance the collaborative and competitive aspects of economic behaviour

With respect to these two goals, both Nations and Corporations have worked competitively, and Nations have protected and encouraged their Corporations to do so. As voters we typically encourage them in the desire to protect our own interests. Our governments walk a tightrope when they do anything against this principle because they risk or are seen to risk your job, your level of prosperity and mine.

Ultimately though this has led to exploitation of weaker economies by stronger ones. It has brought some very mixed messages around the use of international aid, documented in the 1970's under the book title "Aid as Imperialism". Collectively we want to give to the poor, but not too much and we certainly don't want to give up control.

The lack of global co-ordination prevents us from finding a way out. At a recent UK conference I attended there was strong consensus in the room about the new mechanisms needed in corporate governance but the question repeatedly surfaced regarding how the UK or Europe could do this if others didn't. My question was "what if there are people all over the world coming to the same conclusions?" This is not a problem that will be solved over night and it may only be achievable by degrees, but the balance that exists now often amounts to abuse.

From a more purely self-interested point of view the exploitation makes enemies and creates political conflict which we then incur military expenditure to combat. It is well known that if all our expenditure on weaponry were used for directly productive endeavours we could eliminate global poverty. Our challenge is not that this is naive and idealistic and basically impossible. It is only that we don't know how to achieve it and have not yet begun to take the steps in that direction. There is no denying that there are tensions and hostilities with long histories. Nor can we doubt that there are armaments industries which are happy for fear and tension to persist. Even so there is no sense in throwing petrol on the fires by not pursuing less conflict-generating policies. Swords into ploughshares is an old idea that has been a long time waiting.

Policy must also be honoured by implementation. Agencies working on the delivery of the UN Millennium Development Goals which were intended to halve global poverty by 2015 have been angered by the failure of several of the richer countries to deliver on their funding promises. They are particularly upset that this is blamed on the recession. Considering that the funding shortfall is under $20 billion over a decade and is dwarfed by the hundreds of billions which were found almost overnight to rescue the banking system, one can understand their response.

19) **Balancing stakeholder needs.** We must create supportive legal, governance and financial frameworks to enable corporate cultures to more easily meet the needs of all stakeholders in a balanced way. (See no. 8 above).

In Chapter 8 we addressed the reasons of corporate governance and financial control that apply to achieving stakeholder balance in face of the widely-held belief that putting profits ahead of everything else is the only way to be successful. This is resonant with the Darwinian "competition" myth, where the benefits of co-operative, collaborative and mutually creative approaches are not taken account of.

Michael Strong and John Mackey attack many of the myths about what makes a company successful, and John Mackey is well known for building his two billion dollar "Whole Foods Market" company on collaborative, multi-stakeholder principles. In their book "Be the Solution", they reproduce graphs showing how well the companies which take such approaches can do. Mackey has developed this case further in "Conscious Capitalism" and there are others we will refer to.

Charts like the one below show how the organisations which are rated by employees as "the best to work for" consistently out-perform the S&P500 (US share prices index). Many businesses have come to recognise that customer satisfaction, supplier partnership, employee well-being, community engagement and environmental sustainability can all be contributors to an improved "bottom line", as well as to the ability of the company to withstand difficult times. Raj Sisodia's book "Firms of Endearment" and his collaboration with Mackey also extend these arguments.

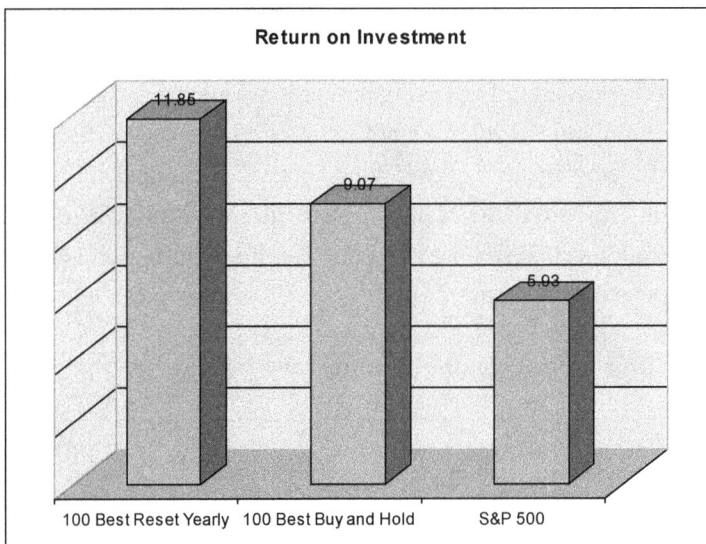

Return on Investment

| 100 Best Reset Yearly | 100 Best Buy and Hold | S&P 500 |

11.85 — 9.07 — 5.03

The attitudes of investors to such long-term viewpoints needs to change as the demand for short-term returns has in many cases prevented companies from operating intelligently. Bonus schemes based on short-term profitability compound this effect and there is evidence that many of these do not even deliver the intended behaviour[xx].

We have already presented Prof. Colin Mayer's "Firm Commitment" which deals at length with the requirement to restore trust in corporations. In due course we will say more about his suggestions for the governance that is required to ensure this. Also mentioned previously, Jon Miller and Lucy Parker travelled the world to harvest inspiring examples of the businesses that are already doing this work, documented in their book "Everybody's business". Some of their examples are of new organisations such as Mahindra which is bringing step by step transformation in of India, particular in the whole platform of how to support small-scale agriculture technically, educationally and financially. Others are of multinationals who are gradually turning around their titanic vessels. Some of the names might confound general expectations – companies like Pepsi-Cola and BHP Billiton - engaging very deeply in multi-stakeholder and "win-win-win" engagements. The route to sustainability and societal enhancement is already being shown to support bottom-line profit.

Both of these books demonstrate that many of the steps towards this balance are already possible. The best companies are adopting them, and even some parts of companies which are not yet seen as the best. The purpose of this goal is to emphasise that we would move faster and more easily in the direction they advocate if there were no constraints in our accounting, taxation and legal systems to prevent it. This in turn might encourage more others to take such steps

Connecting Values, goals and monetary Value

[xx] Management Rewired : Charles S. Jacobs

20) **Costs and benefits are not all material.** We must develop the capability to recognise and assess costs and benefits at both material and non-material levels.

21) **Living Systems have Value.** We must extend our ability to ascribe monetary value in a way that encompasses living systems – that it is assumed that every species and ecosystem has financial worth even where we have not yet discovered it or measured it in human terms.

22) **The Environment has Value.** We must improve our systems for recognising the financial cost of environmental impact, extending beyond toxicity, atmospheric and habitat damage to include the sensed aspect of contribution to our quality of life and that of future generations.

23) **True Cost Accounting.** We must not continue to externalise costs to be left unpaid or picked up at random by others and by society. Our financial thinking about the cost of goods must recognise fully not only the cost of manufacture, but the cost of packaging, package disposal, recycling, the economics of repair and non-repair. We must account for cost of final disposal where we fail in those others.

24) **Full cost raw materials recognition.** Enhance our financial thinking and systems to recognise the true cost of raw materials – the environmental costs of obtaining them, the impact on inhabitants of source regions, the cost of proper management of toxic wastes from refining them and the subsequent recovery of exploited areas.

Human Values and the need for a responsive strategy

The five goals above are presented in recognition of the fact that as yet we have not been good at ascribing monetary value in all areas where human value exists. Most people would agree that happiness is an important human value. In varying degrees, the same could be said of community, environmental beauty, care for other creatures. Even before we began to recognise that we are in many cases dependent on nature and the non-material world, before we could ascribe a cost to the ill-health effects of stress or the indirect costs of family breakdown, we knew that these things were important to us and would express them in varying forms in our collective Values systems. We don't yet have the ability to join these up on a balance sheet or national budget.

By way of illustration, I heard on the radio recently that whenever a judge looks at the choice of sending a criminal to jail, or of offering some alternative and potentially remedial treatment (such as drug dependency support) the playing field is tilted by the system. There is always a budget for incarceration because that is a national provision. But if the judge believes that a non-custodial alternative would be better, and even if they know from experience that it would be cheaper, the money is not guaranteed to be there. This is because such provision is typically local, and budgets have to be found. The result is excessive prison numbers, loss of opportunity to treat and higher re-offending rates. We need systems which are adequate to the complexity of our problems and to the many costs which are indirect, or hard to gauge.

Lester Brown's book "Plan B" focuses strongly on the global costs of such failures and their impact on our future. His focus is particularly towards our management of our relationship with natural resources and the danger to food security. His analysis is deep, comprehensive and offers solutions which are well beyond the scope of this book. But he too is calling for a different attitude to monetary value. Here are examples he gives around our financial attitude to oil.

One of the best examples of this massive market failure can be seen in the United States, where the gasoline pump price was around $3 per gallon in mid-2009. This reflects only the cost of finding the oil, pumping it to the surface, refining it into gasoline, and delivering the gas to service stations. It overlooks the costs of climate change as well as the costs of tax subsidies to the oil industry (such as the U.S. oil depletion allowance), the burgeoning military costs of protecting access to oil in the politically unstable Middle East, and the health care costs of treating respiratory illnesses from breathing polluted air.

Based on a study by the International Center for Technology Assessment, these costs now total nearly $12 per gallon ($3.17 per liter) of gasoline burned in the

United States. If these were added to the $3 direct cost of the gasoline, motorists would pay $15 a gallon for gas at the pump. In reality, burning gasoline is very costly, but the market tells us it is cheap, thus grossly distorting the structure of the economy.

A similar situation exists with food. If we paid the full cost of producing it— including the true cost of the oil used, the future costs of overpumping aquifers, the destruction of land through erosion and the carbon dioxide emissions from land clearing—food would cost far more than we now pay for it in the supermarket.

Lester Brown's analysis is an exceptionally brilliant example of what is required if we are to manage our way out of our current situation. It calls for the same shift of attitudes and requires the underpinning of an economic system that enables us to embed the new set of Values. It provides a new perspective on what it means to fight poverty. It is also affordable and achievable. Our challenge is to mobilise his vision.

25) **Planetary stewardship.** Develop systems which ensure and enforce that ownership of, control over or material benefit from any natural planetary resource is closely coupled with its stewardship; recognising that none of us own the Earth or its riches, that we are at best co-tenants and joint beneficiaries.

There is a saying "live as if you would die tomorrow, farm as if you would live forever". It is hard to argue with the concept that the Earth's resources are gifts (from God or from life) which are not just for us but for future generations. It is hard to provide a moral argument why those gifts should be owned by anyone for their special benefit – beyond the right of individuals to have some security in respect of their dwelling. We accept this geographical lottery in respect of oil, potash, aluminium, diamonds and even water, largely because it has always been so. Potentially we have the option to make a conscious choice. This might be a less wasteful use of human energy than fighting wars over them.

Most of the history of ownership has been based on conquest, hierarchy and patronage. Of course there have been landowners who recognised their obligations as stewards of the land for the future, who improved their estates and who also recognised their duty to people in their communities, and who ensured that the sick and old were cared for. But there were many who didn't, and the novels of Jane Austen or Elizabeth Gaskell could provide plentiful examples. This can be contrasted with almost any Stage 2 tribal society, where stewardship would not be optional; immediate dependency on the land and its creatures would make it a matter of survival. While ownership is now considered normal, we instinctively recognise the truth that "the Earth does not belong to man: man belongs to the Earth". Globally we are now in the position of stage 2 tribes. Our survival depends on collective recognition and enforcement of this truth.

26) **True National benefit assessment.** We need to replace monetary measures of national success (such as GDP) with measurement that also assesses physical health, social, cultural and spiritual well-being, community strength and cohesion, habitat quality, human longevity and systemic sustainability.

Such measures are already partly developed, such as the UN supported Human Development Index (which is weighted heavily towards education) and the happy planet index, which is backed by Friends of the Earth among others, and has a stronger ecological component. The Calvert-Henderson Quality of Life indicators may come close to meeting the above targets.

27) **True National Cost recognition.** We require the ability to distinguish economically between activities which are productive (such as agriculture and manufacture) and activities which however essential represent human costs such courts, prisons, hospitals, social care, waste management and insurance claims We must measure both Gross Domestic Product and Gross Domestic "Cost".

There is a conventional view that you can't manage what you don't measure. This is literally true in many areas. Here it shades more towards a blend with metaphorical truth. We have not valued the planet and its finite resources. We have not valued the living environment for its functional importance or its contribution to the human soul. We use money to value our "prosperity" but are unable to ascribe value to our happiness or our health. If you have a heart attack due to high stress levels your healthcare costs will be added to the Gross National Product. The wealth from which you paid for it would count as your prosperity.

We have not valued many of these things but even when we do we have not been able to measure them, or at least assess them in such a way that they affect our view of what is "profitable". Only when we force them to be valued will they affect governance choices as much as is needed. In some areas, only when we can ascribe financial costs will we be able to ensure that polluters pay what they must, and that they have an incentive to reduce the damage they cause. Only when we are able to factor in the costs of diminishing resources will there be full incentive to ensure that there is investment in their substitutes. In many areas costs are being externalised and are falling on taxpayers – like the costs of landfill for packaging disposal. Corporations would improve faster if such costs were not externalised, but instead became an item in market competitiveness.

28) **Improve our thinking around inflation and growth.** We must reduce systems and activities which embed monetary inflation as an inevitable feature of economic life and assume that our children and grandchildren will pick up the bill. This requires us to learn to distinguish natural and systemic planetary growth from the growth of money supply.

Beneath this proposal is a hornet's nest of mythologies and economic conventions whose result is that governments are not able to act in our interests. That statement is true at a purely economic level; they cannot take care of our money. It is also true at the level of planetary health. Their viewpoints oblige them to pursue policies which are unsustainable.

Once again I draw on the analysis provided by James Rickards (see item 12 above). His thesis begins with the assertion that the US economy has failed to deliver the robust recovery that policy makers were awaiting. Central to his book is the view that current economic problems are structural, not cyclical and that the US is technically in a depression, which Keynes defined as "a chronic condition of sub-normal activity for a considerable period without any marked tendency either towards recovery or towards complete collapse." He provides data to counter the regular government assertion of

187

improvements – including the fact that claimed job creation has been in 60% of cases in the lowest-earning sectors of the economy (twice the usual proportion) and in many cases were short-hours working. The percentage of Americans in the work force had not increased but rather had dropped from 66% to 63.5%. Meanwhile 50 million people are dependent on food stamps. The same symptoms are evident in the UK, where food banks have become essential for very many people, and austerity measures threaten to intensify this.

The economic convention in these conditions is for there to be deflation – that is, that prices decline as businesses sell assets and reduce stocks. Declining prices equates to less money being required to buy available goods – thus the value of money is increasing. We have spent so many decades worrying about inflation that we aren't used to this, and we still aren't worrying because the deflation is masked. Because of massive money printing (QE) there is more money available, and its value is reduced. Deflation means that money moves more slowly, but money-printing means that there is more money circulating – or at least enough to disguise the sluggishness of the economy and to artificially inflate asset prices such as houses and stockmarkets.

So how does this relate to governments? You might think that deflation would be in their interest. Wouldn't they want things to cost less too, for them and us? Unfortunately not. Here's why.

If there is inflation and your wages go up, they get a slice of that increase from your extra tax contributions. If prices go down, your taxes stay the same.

If there is inflation the value of government debt can be paid in less valuable money. In deflation the real value of the debt increases.

If the economy deflates GDP drops. Relative to GDP, debt is higher, so the debt to GDP ratio looks worse (higher risk), which increases the cost of future borrowing.

188

Deflation increases the systemic risk in the banking sector because there is less value in the assets that secure lenders claims against borrowers. Inflation props up the banks and helps keep everyone solvent.

Now, look at this alongside the question of growth. We already know that our resource usage is higher than the planet can sustain. Deflation would assist with this challenge. We could take advantage of the opportunity to slow down and give ourselves more time to deal with the known challenges. This too borders on heresy, both in public policy and in corporate expectations.

29) **Corporate stewardship.** Treat shareholders as suppliers of capital rather than as owners of the enterprise and require that their attitude to the corporation is one of long-term stewardship

In "Firm Commitment" Colin Mayer makes a strong case that one of the improved vehicles for corporate governance should be "In Trust" firms. This form enables the corporation to have shares registered for a number of years of ownership. Voting rights are then made proportional for the number of years for which that share will continue to be owned. Short-term shareholders have more limited voting powers.

Sudhakar Ram makes a similar case to Mayer for improved governance, saying *"In my view governance is a more powerful and comprehensive mechanism that can apply broad principles to policymaking and strategic decisions"* The Trust structure also potentially creates greater separation between governance – the upholding of the firm's values - and senior management / directors – who are responsible for running the enterprise. Shareholders may elect either or both layers. There are many possible variations but we cite this proposal, described in more detail in the book's appendix, as an example of ways to deal with the problems described in Chapter 8, improving corporate stewardship and increasing trust in it.

29) **Corporate legal responsibility**. Corporations are not persons. They need to be legally distinct entities and to have commercial rights but they must not be treated legally as if they have the same rights as individual humans.

30) **Preventive thinking.** We require increased ability to distinguish and assign value to costs incurred (investments in quality) which inhibit later costs; for example between health systems to treat sickness and health systems to maintain wellness.

In determining project viability there are financial measurements like Return on Investment and Net Present Value that are used to quantify whether the investment is worthwhile. Financially these are often weak and usually distorted by the assumptions that are made in order to justify the project.

Nevertheless we have a concept of making long-term decisions for return on investment. We seem not to apply them in public policy. We would apparently rather spend money imprisoning minor criminals than in the education and social policies that would have kept them from crime. Decisions are driven by short-term financial perspectives and shaped by politics more than by genuine analysis.

31) **Governmental long-term responsibilities**. For the sake of ourselves and our children we must require governments to enumerate and be accountable for consequences of their decisions beyond their term of office.

32) **Recognising societal benefit.** We need to move away from the simple division between "for profit" and "not-for-profit" activities, reducing the discrepancies in value assigned between those who work for the benefit of others and those who work to gain benefit from others. We must reduce the devaluation of the former and the change way that teachers, nurses and social carers are viewed economically as a cost to society.

33) **Balance Freedom and Responsibility** Improve our societal capacity to tell the difference between the inalienable value of individual freedom and the right to be socially or environmentally destructive.

Freedom stops at the point where it does tangible harm to others.

34) **Socially responsible valuing of risk.** Create systems which direct the human impulse to gamble and to play with risk towards productive outcomes and away from destructive ones

Freedom to take risk should be protected short of actively self-destructive and societally damaging outcomes.

35) **Right-scale Distributed Democracy.** We need to improve the balance between centralised and locally accountable decision-making.

In most Western countries decision-making is over-centralised. The European Union is under attack because it has failed to find the balance between raising standards and harmonising principles as compared with central control of detail. Reduced centralisation will increase relevance of decisions to local conditions, supporting productive economy and closer attention to cost management. It will also increase engagement with the democratic process and undermine the paralysis of party-based systems.

The reality that we all recognise is that participation in party-based democracy is minimal, voting is increasingly seen as irrelevant and people are alienated from the decision-making that they are governed by. To quote Sudhakar Ram in "The Connected Age"

"Today we take governments for granted and assume democracy is the highest possible form of evolution in terms of government. Has this 200-year-old product of human imagination really reached the highest level of perfection? Is it a system that can take us through the next few centuries?"

Sudhakar recognises the principle of subsidiarity. This is the idea that a central government should perform only those tasks that cannot be performed effectively at a more immediate or local level. It assumes that power is and should be available primarily to the lowest level and ceded only when the task is better performed from a higher level.

He goes on to list the consequences of the assumption that democracy is a peak invention and to recommend the directions that we should move in based on William Nanda Bissell's book "Making India Work". There is no visible reason why the four principles and the ways of implementation that Bissell describes would not work elsewhere. These principles are:-

- Scaled-down government
- Ending poverty (this is not just an Indian problem)
- Simplifying taxation (doesn't everyone want this?)
- Valuing Real Cost.

No doubt other goals will be added to this manifesto, and many will require expansion and change of detail. The purpose here is to put the overall thinking and principle into the public domain and it is assumed in practice that such ideas, wherever they are accepted, will be made manifest in many and varied proposals over a period of time. It is not essential that you agree with all of them, or with every element of detail. What matters is that you can see the need for this breadth of intention to be encompassed in our money systems if we are to have a coherent way forward which holds the many tensions in balance.

Postscript: System Reset

"When any of us meet someone who rejects dominant norms and values, we feel a little less crazy for doing the same. Any act of rebellion or non-participation, even on a very small scale, is therefore a political act."

" The More Beautiful World Our Hearts Know is Possible" Charles Eisenstein

Re-planting the Garden

I have held back from proposing any specific actions in the body of this book. For four years I have hoped that something would emerge from others who are more specialised and trained than I am in the world of economics. My involvement in money comes out of my interest in why things had gone so badly wrong, approached with the mentality of someone who is or has been variously an applications engineer, a change manager, an organisational development specialist, a leadership coach and trainer, resting finally on the bedrock of scientific training and couched in decades of work on my own thinking and feeling systems.

I have come to realise that this odd portfolio causes me to approach questions in a way that few others do. The list of goals displays my profound belief that the world needs comprehensive answers that address all the many aspects of the crisis. There are many smart people who have one of the pieces of this puzzle and who are expert in their own areas. There are some deeply heart-led and spiritually motivated people addressing aspects of our connectedness and our ability to feel as well as analyse what the planet needs. However, I see the need for some joined-up conversations; if they are happening, they are not visible to me. Several years on from the crunch there is more being said about what is wrong than about what will put things right.

I have been watching the world's dramas, amazed at the ability we have to cobble together last-minute fixes and taken aback that the inevitable crash has been held at bay for so long. The problems shift from country to country as one leak after another is plugged but the system remains pressurised and liable to burst. This is inevitable because the problems are too deep, too interconnected and too global to solve. I think it possible that it is only the terror of what happens if this fact is admitted that prevents the full realisation. In any other context this would be called Denial. Even so, some commentators who are not known for alarmism have been publicly using words like "close to Armageddon". So we need some answers very urgently.

I have made it clear that I don't think that pain can be avoided, but how much pain must we experience? If we do not have a vision in place of what is required to emerge from that pain, the disappointment, fear and anger will explode destructively. If we do not have a plan, a serious crisis could turn into a catastrophe.

The plan we need must look vastly different from our past. It cannot be delivered by the bankers and financiers. Even if they avoid being torn apart by mobs they will not be trusted to be either competent or morally sound. It may not even be possible for our governments to deliver it, unless they quickly demonstrate that their efforts to date indicate something other than incompetence. Few economists show the ability to think outside of the box either. Perhaps a few who can demonstrate fully (rather than merely claim) that they saw these problems before 2008 will be capable of assisting the formulation of a solution.

I am not a pessimist. I have considerable faith in our human capacities and my version of the spiritual realm is a loving and supportive one. I also believe that the solutions we need are already present. Lester Brown's Plan B is just one example of this, and organisations like Positive Money, SIMPOL, Reinventing ("Teal") Organisations and Conscious Capitalism have pieces of the solution. If this crisis were to be treated to the same focus, resources and priority as are given to the war on terrorism it would not take long. It might even help the latter too.

This may seem to fly in the face of experience when blatant and corrupt self-interest has undermined so many previous efforts in critical areas like climate change. Regrettably it seems probable that we need a further breakdown in order to shake loose these vested interests and get back the level of shared power that allows the majority interest to be served. The illusion about money is still well in place. Analysts on the daily news programs continue to utter the "growth" mantra as if it might even be possible to generate sufficient to repay what we have borrowed. They oscillate between the perspectives that governments must stop their deficits and the simultaneous knowledge that this means no surplus money to generate the expansion they perceive as the only way in which to make the numbers eventually come right. It's a square that cannot be circled.

Perversely, even though a major debtor country cannot possibly earn enough to settle its debts, on paper it still suits the interests of a bank which holds that debt to lend more to it now. The higher the interest on that new loan the better, because the new asset that is created then appears to more than cover the past exposure. Due to increased risk the new interest rates will be higher than the old ones, so internally the bank will appear to be in good financial shape. They are of course aware of the risk, but on paper writing off the debt looks worse. Issuing new debt keeps the wheels turning for a little while longer, and that is all they know how to do. They can pretend to themselves that the risk is being managed by taking out insurance against default. They seem not to understand that if that kind of default happens, the insurers too, will run out of funds. Who will insure the insurers? Each "solution" you hear of to some crisis or another amounts to just one thing. Someone has agreed to advance more fantasy money in order to postpone the day of reckoning.

Denial is not serving us. While it keeps most banks going and most governments in power it does damage to everyone else. Some countries appear to be emerging as the QE money trickles through, but many businesses remain vulnerable. Families are under stress and insecure. More jobs seem to be created, but more of them are temporary, part-time and lower-paid than is acknowledged. Money continues to flow from the poor and middle-income groups into the pockets of those who continue to exploit the weaknesses of the system. Our futures are mortgaged to the hilt, and every day there is more to put right.

So what's the solution?

At the opening of this book, we imagined what would happen if all the money disappeared. Since then we have been learning the nature of the illusion we live in, which gives a spurious kind of reality to money. The good news is that since this debt money lacks real-world value, we could also write off the debts tomorrow and most of us would not know the difference. The global economy has been pumped up year on year like an over-inflated balloon. We could let the air out and the balloon would still be intact. Surely this is better than continuing to pump until it explodes? For instance it has been suggested that reducing the value of all debts, whether personal, corporate or national, by (say) 50% would immediately reduce some of the damage done by years of debt money.

This may sound too simple, as indeed it is, but think about it just to get a feel for the principle. If the world declares itself bankrupt, subsistence farmers worldwide will not feel it. The slum dwellers in Mumbai will be oblivious. If we tore up all the Credit Default Swaps, Collateralised Debt Obligations and other paper-only financial instruments, only the financial institutions would notice. If all the computers which keep track of the amounts of big debt money were to have their memories wiped, who would be affected? It would be the banks, and those individuals with the biggest amounts of surplus cash who would notice most. The world has already learned how this is done. It goes under the delightful term "haircut".

If something like this does not happen the alternative is liable to be the "Cyprus solution". As far back as in 2009 – 2010, when the ways out of the global crisis were discussed at international summits (G7, G8, G20 and other structures), non-standard ways of banks rescue in contingency were part of the agenda, including the schemes of bailing them out at the expense of account holders.

In March 2013 this happened in Cyprus. It was presented as an ad-libbed decision on the part of the European Union carried out by Cyprus government, a one-time action under the pressure of circumstances. There are those who view it as a test for the future and with good reason. The economics committee of the European Union has voted that this power should be legislated to take effect in 2016. In some measure it would have the same effect as the "haircut" and the proposal is that it would apply to any account with a balance in excess of 100,000 Euros. The danger is that it works merely to prop up the banks, does not deal with the mountain of paper debt, is clumsy and unfair and works strongly against the interests of the mass of the population.

I am not suggesting that the "haircut" solution is precisely what should happen. Of course it is over-simplified. But the details could be worked on. It is important that we recognise that it is our view of the money which creates the problem and not the money by itself. We have not been looking at what matters and what doesn't. We have focussed on the money and not on happiness, health, well-being and mutual care. What would happen if we worked on the details from a perspective of what really matters?

So what does matter?

The well-being of individuals and families matters. It is important to protect our savings to the extent necessary to meet our needs, including those who have saved for pensions, or who are funding health and elder care.

It is important to keep our agriculture, industries and services running.

We will want healthcare and education to remain operational.

We have to preserve the real economy. Investments in it (shares etc.) need to be kept intact. Debts for real goods and services already incurred or contracted for may need to be honoured in order that companies stay afloat.

We need banks, in the old-fashioned sense of organisations that take care of our stored money. Much of this function can now be performed by a wide variety of institutions, many of them on-line. We do not need to preserve the vast infrastructure of paper transaction churning and fantasy investment activity. We need to get back to financial basics. The Cyprus solution puts the banks first. That is not what we need – quite the reverse.

The goal of this exercise is to bring the economy back into "present time". It is a system reset, a global reboot. The money that we live from and use to keep the wheels turning matters. Debts that can never and will never be repaid anyway don't matter – so let's get real about that and stop kicking the can down the road. If banks everywhere have to write off some numbers it is not a big deal. The numbers weren't real anyway – they were figments of a collective imagination, promises of future activity. Guess what? The future can be changed. In fact it already is changing. The question is, are we?

If the collapse is inevitable then we have two choices. We can let it happen to us with the result that companies close. We can watch the banks be wiped out, taking our savings with them. We can witness the complete chaos and breakdown that would follow when planes and trucks stop moving and food supplies don't enter cities. We could have a 1929 scenario with a probable aftermath to match.

Alternatively we can manage the collapse. We can fix the unreal economy, tear up or re-value imaginary and doubtful assets as necessary. We can protect that which must be protected and let go of that which does not serve our collective human future. I do not suggest that this will feel easy. There will be much to let go of. It is likely that the more we have beyond that which is tangible (like cars and houses) or locally held (like cash and personal accounts) or lodged in real investments (like company shares) the more we may have to lose. But when we move beyond what is tangible the majority of what is lost will be on paper. This will probably damage pension funds and require a major rethink of how we care for the elderly, but that is nothing new. This will sometimes be as unfair as losing your house to a bomb during wartime and will demand the same degree of collective ability to pull together and take care of those who are genuinely hurt. But surely this collateral damage is a better choice than the kind of chaos where we tear each other apart.

And then we will need to build a new economy. The criteria for that exercise have been laid out above. We will need to learn what previous generations considered normal – to live within our means, to borrow in order to increase capacity rather than consumption, or to cope with emergencies.

We will need to find appropriate blends and balances - freedom to achieve alongside fairness, incentive to create alongside support for those less fortunate. Put simply, we will have to behave like communities, at local, national and global levels. We know how to do this for short periods as we did when Live Aid was taking place and as many are doing now through micro-loan systems and credit unions. We will need to learn how to make it part of our way of life.

198

Those who still have much will need to find some old values of service, contribution, responsibility to those less fortunate and pride in the achievement of philanthropy. Bill Gates and Warren Buffet have set an example already. Conspicuous consumption should become a matter for shame and some of our celebrities should begin to feel our distaste more than our envy and admiration.

A precursor to this book was called "Future Money". That title reflected the calls for us to create a new set of relationships with money and the sense of looking forward. Less obviously, it represented the way we have been in recent decades, living off our own futures, spending money that we had not yet created. But we are here, the goods have been bought, the services delivered. We made promises to pay which we can all agree to break. The proposals made in this book prepare the ground for our new relationships with each other and for our new relationship with money. If we avoid collapse, then they will help create a more stable future. If we don't then we will need them as part of our recovery. As Dr Don Beck is fond of observing, there are no more prizes for forecasting the rain, only for building the ark. The clouds are on the horizon. Either way, it is time to engage.

Jon Freeman

October 2015

Acknowledgements

I have to start with recognition of Professor Clare W. Graves. While Watson, Crick and Franklin were unravelling the structural mysteries of DNA, Clare Graves was busy decoding the secrets of our social and psychological development. He is the Darwin of our cultural evolution.

Closely following him is Dr Don E. Beck, who has developed what Graves started in its theoretical richness, its communicability and its applications. I encountered SDi long after Graves' death but am very grateful to have known Don personally for several years and I owe a lot to his insight, wisdom and encouragement.

Said Dawlabani has already received special mention in the text. His presentation in 2009 about the derivatives mess and the Values systems that propelled it were another trigger. As noted, "Memenomics", the book which eventually followed took his initial ideas wide and deep. Our different directions of travel led us to see the same diamond, but through different facets.

Louis Böhtlingk's vision of a "Care-First" world and his articulation of the inner transition that we are making triggered the writing of this book, taking my interest in finance off the back-burner.. He had the *mythos* of the change, to which this book supplies the *logos.* The content began to formulate itself as I explained the Spiral and the outer world to him.

Since then many others have contributed directly or indirectly to the thinking, or read the manuscript in draft. Since I did not always follow advice I own any weaknesses or errors that remain. The personal list includes Eoin McCarthy, Jordan Macleod, Marcos Frangos, Roger Wetzel, David Kapfer and Sarah Cowell. Heather Cowen, Quentin Cowen and Gabriella Kapfer also shared in aspects of the inner journey into the mystery of money, and have given their support.

The writers and speakers who have helped my thinking develop are visible in the text. John Mackey, Raj Sisodia, Sudhakar Ram, Richard Barrett and Colin Mayer have all been influential and several of them have also helped make the UK Chapter of Conscious Capitalism a reality. More recently I have greatly appreciated the work of Charles Eisenstein, Frederic Laloux, James Rickards and Edouard Dommen.

My colleagues and co-directors in that chapter have all been supportive and I must give particular mention to Gina Hayden. In other groups such as Spirit at Work and the UK Values Alliance are many more gifted, caring and clever people, the ones who are equipped to support the implementation of the ideas in this book. To those I add Cindy Wigglesworth, developer of Spiritual Intelligence and author of "SQ21", and the community of Deep Change practitioners who are around her. Then there are the other SDi colleagues who constitute the Global Centre for Human Emergence. All these groups are fine examples for the collaborative age.

I am grateful for the review comments and supportive endorsements received as this book was prepared for publication.

Like all authors who live alongside others, my last acknowledgements are in life terms the first. When writing "The Science of Possibility" Juliana Freeman was an inspiration and editorial partner. Similarly she shared the exploration of our inner worlds in relation to money. Her contributions to the first version of this book were many, both through her love and care and through her healing capabilities which kept workaholic burn-out at bay. Juliana and I are still close friends and collaborators, supported by her wife-to-be, Yvonne. Sophia Wilding also gave considerable love, support and care. Both fed me and reminded me in word and being that I have a heart as well as a brain.

Appendix: Spiral Dynamics Integral

Spiral Dynamics is a much deeper and richer theory than is conveyed in this book. Many aspects of its application are explored on the CHE-UK website, which also contains free downloadable resources from Don Beck and others.

Seeing Graves' theory to be the equivalent for socio-psychological development of Darwin's theory for biological evolution could sound like extravagant hyperbole, but it is meant seriously. Just as those who understand cancer hope that genetic knowledge will provide a solution, we see in SDi the cures for social ills, organisational failures and international conflicts. Don Beck's passion has led him into South Africa and Palestine to assist in developing solutions. Thus the application of the theory to our economic development is just one facet among many and the work of our CHE colleagues in the Netherlands in sustainability, of CHE Canada (Marilyn Hamilton) on cities and of CHE Mid-east (Elza Maalouf and Said Dawlabani) on development in that region are further examples of practical application.

This variety and depth should be seen as indicating just how extensive the theory can be. It is not a typology describing different kinds of people. The Values systems (which were called stages in this presentation) are points on a continuum in which the dynamics of why and how people shift from one to another have more significance than where they are today. Understanding those dynamics, and the different ways in which Values may present themselves is both an art and a science. Knowing how this works offers keys that unlock solutions in just about all areas of human behaviour – individual, organisational and national.

If the glimpse of SDi in this book encourages others to learn more of this theory and its capacity to support the changes humanity needs, that would be bonus.

Introductory Video on Spiral Dynamics:

http:/www.scienceofpossibility.net/sdintro.html

About the Author

Jon Freeman always wanted to understand how the world worked. This led him to study Philosophy and Psychology which didn't provide many answers and then Human Sciences which provided a few.

Narrowly avoiding an academic career through blessed failure of self-discipline, he was drawn into the rising world of Information Technology, where the design of integrated applications at least helped in making companies work and led to a career in management and consultancy which connected systems understanding to the management of human change.

Inevitably, the need to explore the world could not be kept entirely at bay, and nearly four decades of exploration into personal development, alternative approaches to healing, stress management and the study of human sexuality and relationships took place in parallel. This led to a second-string career in personal coaching, workshop leading and teaching intuition skills. Some of the experiences along this road demanded a view of science which adequately explains an intuitive, psychic and spiritual reality, as documented in "The Science of Possibility". Further details can be found on www.spiralworld.net and www.scienceofpossibility.net .

These explorations also led to a "chance" meeting with Dr Don Beck, and to the recognition that all the answers Jon had looked for would have been available during his time at university, if only he had been told then about Clare W. Graves. Better late than never, he is now a Senior Practitioner and trainer in Spiral Dynamics Integral working as a mentor in organisational development, design and leadership. Writing books reflects a passion for communicating ideas which also extends to public speaking.

In what remains of his time, Jon listens to music of many kinds, reads avidly, watches movies and is a Trustee of a local charity.

References and resources

Spiral Dynamics - Mastering Values, Leadership and Change. Don Beck and Christopher Cowan, 1996. Blackwell Publishing, ISBN 1-55786-940-5

The Crucible – Forging South Africa's Future in search of a template for the world. Don Beck and Graham Linscott. 1991. Most recent publication by Coera.us, ISBN 978-0-9640026-2-3

Be the Solution – How Entrepreneurs and Conscious Capitalists can solve all the world's problems. Michael Strong and John Mackey 2009. John Wiley and Sons. ISBN 978-0-470-45003-1

Conscious Capitalism. John Mackey and Raj Sisodia. Harvard Business School Press 2013. ISBN 978-1-4221-4420-6

Memenomics: The next generation economic system. Said Elias Dawlabani. Select Books Inc. 2013 ISBN 978-1-5907-9996-3

The Connected Age: Sudhakar Ram. Collins Business 2014. ISBN 978-93-5136-199-2

Firm Commitment. Colin Mayer. Oxford University Press 2013. ISBN 978-0 1996-6993-6

Everybody's Business: Jon Miller and Lucy Parker. Biteback Publishing 2013. ISBN 978-1-8495-4608-9

The Values Driven Organisation. Richard Barrett Routledge 2014. ISBN 978-0-4158-1503-1

New Currency – How money changes the world as we know it. Jordan Bruce Macleod, 2009. Integral Publishers, ISBN: 978-0-615-27612-0

Integral Consciousness and the Future of Evolution. Steve McIntosh, 2007. Paragon House ISBN: 978-1-55778-867-2

Davies, Glyn. A history of money from ancient times to the present day, 3rd ed. Cardiff: University of Wales Press, 2002. ISBN 0-7083-1717-0.

The Collapse of Complex Societies. Prof. Joseph Tainter, 1990. Cambridge University Press ISBN: 978-0521386739

The Free Market and Its Enemies; Pseudo-Science, Socialism, and Inflation. Ludwig von Mises, 1951. Foundation for Economic Education ISBN: 978-1153483117

Plan B – Mobilising to save civilization. Lester R Brown. W. W. Norton & Co.; Revised edition (23 Oct 2009) ISBN: 978-0393337198 http://www.earth-policy.org/images/uploads/book_files/pb4book.pdf

Firms of Endearment. Raj Sisodia and others. Pearson Prentice Hall ISBN: 978-0131873728

SQ21: The 21 skills of Spiritual Intelligence. Cindy Wigglesworth. Select Books Inc. 2012. ISBN 978-1-5907-9235-3

The Science of Possibility. Jon Freeman, 2014 Spiralworld ISBN 978-0-956-0107-3-5

Dare to Care. Louis Böhtlingk: Cosimo Publishing 2011 ISBN: 978-1616405502

The Death of Money. James Rickards, Portfolio / Penguin 2014. ISBN:-978-1591846703

A Peaceable Economy. Edouard Dommen World Council of Churches 2014. ISBN: 978-2825416396

Web Resources

Introductory Video on Spiral Dynamics:

http:/www.scienceofpossibility.net/sdintro.html

Louis Böhtlingk: www.carefirstworld.com

www.positivemoney.org

www.slowmoney.org

Don Beck, Spiral Dynamics: www.spiraldynamics.net

Don Beck, Centre for Human Emergence: www.humanemergence.org

Other CHEs

United Kingdom: www.humanemergence.org.uk

Middle-East: http://www.humanemergencemiddleeast.org

Netherlands: www.humanemergence.nl

Canada: www.humanemergence.ca

Chile: www.emergerhumano.org

Jon Freeman: www.spiralfutures.com (Consultancy)
                  www.jonfreeman.co.uk (Portfolio)
                  www.spiralworld.net   (Publishing)
                  www.scienceofpossibility.net (Science of Consciousness)

Jordan MacLeod in Kosmos Journal:
http://www.newcurrency.org/blog/circulation-charge/hello-world/#more-1

www.ingramcontent.com/pod-product-compliance
Lightning Source LLC
Chambersburg PA
CBHW060555220326
41598CB00024B/3114